ASHLEY CULLEN

From Skyscrapers to Stables

First edition

This book was professionally typeset on Reedsy.
Find out more at reedsy.com

Contents

1 A Sudden Return 1
2 Unwanted Responsibility 7
3 The Man in the Stables 12
4 Old Wounds and New Struggles 18
5 Uneasy Beginnings 24
6 The Memory of Home 31
7 Unexpected Help 37
8 The Hidden Pain 43
9 Conflict at the Heart of the Ranch 50
10 A Glimpse of Vulnerability 57
11 The Inherited Burden 64
12 The Unraveling 70
13 Secrets in the Barn 76
14 A Test of Trust 81
15 The Tension Builds 87
16 Crossing the Line 93
17 The First Kiss 99
18 Rebuilding Bridges 105
19 The Pressure Grows 111
20 Confessions of the Heart 116
21 The Last Offer 121
22 The Unspoken Future 127
23 A Fork in the Road 133
24 A Moment of Clarity 139

25	The Decision	144
26	The Cost of Change	149
27	The Family Reunion	155
28	The Final Test	161
29	New Beginnings	166
30	The Heart's Choice	172
31	The Legacy Restored	178
32	The Simple Life	184
33	A Forever Love	189
34	The Final Chapter	194
35	From Skyscrapers to Stables	199

1

A Sudden Return

Amelia Pierce stood at the floor-to-ceiling window of her high-rise office, gazing out at the bustling city below. The skyline of towering glass structures stretched out in every direction, a sea of lights shimmering against the fading daylight. Her reflection in the glass was sharp and focused, just as she had always been—a woman who knew exactly what she wanted and how to get it.

But today, there was a strange heaviness in the air. The phone call she had received earlier weighed on her mind, a sudden disturbance to the carefully crafted life she had built. Her father was dead. A heart attack, the message had said, was unexpected. The estate—her family's estate—needed her.

She'd never expected this call. Never expected to be dragged back to the place she had left so many years ago. She had left the country house behind intending to never return. The memories there—her mother's death, her father's overwhelming expectations, the relentless pursuit of a life she never truly wanted—

had left scars that ran deeper than anyone could understand. Yet, here she was, on the verge of having to face them all again.

"Miss Pierce, the car's ready," her assistant, Emily, called from the doorway, breaking through her reverie. Amelia didn't turn to acknowledge her. Instead, she simply nodded, her thoughts swirling in a hundred different directions.

Her fingers hovered over her phone for a moment, checking the time. Her flight was in an hour, but she wasn't sure how to feel. The duty to her family, to the estate, to the legacy her father had left behind, loomed heavy in her chest. But there was also resentment, a quiet but pervasive feeling that had built up over the years—the kind of resentment that only children of powerful families could truly understand. Her father had always treated her as though she were a mere extension of his will, a pawn in his ever-expanding empire. And now, it seemed that empire had crumbled, and she was the only one left to pick up the pieces.

As she stepped into the sleek black car that would take her to the airport, Amelia stared out the window once again, her thoughts still heavy. The hum of the city's chaos barely registered as her mind drifted to the past, to the place she had escaped from. The Pierce family estate wasn't just a piece of property—it was a symbol of everything she had run from. It was too big, too isolated, too full of ghosts.

The countryside was a world away from the rush of the city, and yet, the minute Amelia stepped off the plane, she could feel the weight of her decision sinking in. The air was heavier here—cool, thick with the scent of the earth. It was a strange contrast to the sterile, polished atmosphere of her New York penthouse. The air smelled of soil, of grass, of the old oaks that had stood at the edges of her family's property for generations.

Amelia adjusted her sunglasses as she stepped down from the plane, the rush of nostalgia and dread hitting her like a wave. The town she'd once known as a quiet, almost idyllic place now felt foreign to her. The memories that had once seemed so distant, so buried, came rushing back with an intensity she hadn't anticipated. The fields stretched out before her like a never-ending sea of green, dotted here and there with the old stone buildings that made up the estate. The house itself—massive and imposing—loomed in the distance, a place that had once felt like home but now felt like a stranger's house, full of shadows and silence.

Her driver, an older man who had worked for her family for years, stood by the car waiting for her, his expression neutral. He didn't offer any comfort, just the quiet understanding that this was a return, not a homecoming.

The drive to the estate felt longer than it ever had before, as if time itself had stretched, waiting for her to face what lay ahead. The silence in the car was deafening, and the only sound was the steady hum of the tires against the country road, the occasional bird call, and the soft rustle of the trees lining the path. Amelia felt the tension tighten in her shoulders as she watched the familiar landmarks pass by. The old church she used to walk past on her way to school, the rusted fence where her childhood dog had escaped all those years ago, the wildflower patches that reminded her of her mother's garden.

Her father's death had brought her back to a place she'd been trying to forget for so long, and yet, it felt impossible to truly leave it behind. Everything about this place was tied to memories—some good, but most painful. The only escape from it had been her career, the endless hours in her office, the deal-making, the contracts. It was easier to shut off the emotions when you were sitting in a boardroom, watching the numbers climb, than to face the complicated mess of family.

As they neared the gates of the estate, Amelia couldn't help but glance out the window, her heart tightening in her chest. The gates, tall and wrought iron, loomed ahead, just as they always had. But today, they felt different—closed off, a barrier to a past that had haunted her for so long.

The house came into view soon after, perched atop a hill, its towering façade casting a long shadow over the grounds. It was a grand structure, built in the style of old-world opulence, with ivy creeping up the stone walls, and windows that looked like dark eyes watching the world. As the car pulled to a stop in front of the massive double doors, Amelia's breath caught in her throat.

The house hadn't changed, not really. But she had. She wasn't the young girl who had once run through these halls with dreams of escape. No, she was a woman now, hardened by the years, shaped by the choices she had made. And yet, as she stood before the door, she felt the same sense of being trapped that had always plagued her when she lived here.

The housekeeper, an older woman named Mrs. Delaney, opened the door and greeted Amelia with a solemn nod. Her face softened as she took in Amelia's appearance, her eyes holding a mixture of sympathy and something darker—something unspoken.

"Miss Pierce," Mrs. Delaney said, her voice low. "It's good to see you again, though I wish the circumstances were different."

Amelia didn't know how to respond, so she simply nodded, following Mrs. Delaney inside. The air inside the house was thick with dust, and the silence felt almost suffocating. The grand staircase, which had once seemed so inviting, now felt like a barrier she didn't want to cross. The memories rushed back—her father's harsh words, the tension at the dinner table, her mother's soft laughter that had been so quickly silenced by her father's commanding presence.

But now, it was just her. And the estate, standing as a monument to her family's legacy, was all she had left.

Amelia walked through the rooms, her footsteps echoing in the vast space. Each room told a story—of wealth, and power, but also of the cracks that had always existed beneath the surface. Her father had built this empire with blood, sweat, and iron will. But in the end, it hadn't been enough. And now, as she stood here, in this place that had once felt like home, she realized she had inherited more than just an estate. She had inherited a broken legacy.

Her father's death had tied her to this place once more, and no matter how much she tried to escape, it would always pull her back. This was where it all began. And now, it was where it would all end.

2

Unwanted Responsibility

Amelia sat in the cold, formal office, her fingers tapping nervously on the polished surface of the wooden desk. The documents before her were clear, precise, and cold—much like everything else about her father's business dealings. She felt a growing sense of unease settle into her chest as the lawyer's voice droned on, explaining the terms of her father's will.

"There's one last stipulation, Miss Pierce," the lawyer, Mr. Henderson, said, his voice thick with formality. "Your father has left the Pierce Family Ranch to you. He has made it clear that you must oversee the operation for a full year. During this time, you will be responsible for making all decisions regarding the ranch's future."

Amelia blinked, not quite comprehending what she was hearing. "Wait... you mean, I have to run the ranch?" she asked, her voice tinged with disbelief.

Mr. Henderson nodded gravely. "That's correct. Your father

believed that you had the skills to make critical decisions about the property, even if it's been some time since you've lived here."

She felt her world shift beneath her feet. Amelia had always known that her father expected great things from her, but this was an entirely new level of responsibility. The Pierce Family Ranch, nestled deep in the heart of the countryside, was a place she had long distanced herself from. It was not her world anymore, and it hadn't been for years. The sprawling property, the stables, the livestock—all of it was a part of the past she had run away from, and she had no desire to return to it.

"Surely there must be someone else—someone with more experience—who can run the ranch," Amelia protested, her frustration mounting. "I'm a lawyer. I deal with contracts, negotiations, not—" She gestured vaguely toward the thick stack of ranching paperwork. "Not this."

Mr. Henderson's expression softened, but his words remained firm. "I'm afraid not, Miss Pierce. Your father's will is very clear. He believed that you, as his only child, were the only one who could take charge of the ranch, especially after he passed. It's your responsibility now."

Sitting back in her chair, Amelia felt the weight of her father's decision settle heavily on her shoulders. She had spent years carving out a life for herself in the fast-paced world of corporate law. She had spent years running away from the pressures of the ranch, from the suffocating legacy of her family, only to return now—unwillingly—to face a responsibility she didn't want.

"You should take some time to read through the documents," Mr. Henderson said, gathering the papers in front of him. "There's a detailed breakdown of the ranch's operations and your responsibilities in here. I'm sure you'll find everything you need to get started."

Amelia barely registered the words as Mr. Henderson handed her the paperwork. Her thoughts were a whirlwind, drowning out the lawyer's voice. How was she supposed to take control of something she knew nothing about? The ranch was so different from the world she had built for herself. She had grown accustomed to the shiny, polished world of skyscrapers and boardrooms, the sound of phones ringing off the hook, and the click of high heels on marble floors. She was not a rancher and never had been. The thought of living among cattle and horses, of making decisions about crop yields and livestock care, was utterly foreign to her.

She looked down at the documents in front of her, the weight of her father's expectations pressing on her chest. There was no escaping this responsibility, no way to deny it. She had no choice but to go through with it, even if it terrified her. With a deep breath, Amelia stood up, took the papers, and nodded to Mr. Henderson.

"I'll go over this," she said, her voice more strained than she intended.

After a brief discussion, Amelia left the lawyer's office, the weight of her new responsibilities following her out the door. The drive back to the Pierce Family Ranch was long and silent. The estate seemed to stretch endlessly before her, a sprawling reminder of the life she had once known and tried so desperately to leave behind. As she approached the large iron gates that marked the entrance to the estate, her stomach tightened.

Amelia had not been back to the ranch in over five years, and the memories of that place—of growing up under the shadow of her father's relentless demands—were still fresh in her mind. She remembered her mother's absence, the empty feeling of the house after her mother had died, and the way her father's coldness had grown in proportion to his expectations for her. It was a place of suffocating perfection, where emotions were measured by success and failure. It was a world where her every move had been scrutinized, and where her only worth had been in meeting her father's high standards.

The car finally pulled to a stop in front of the old, grandiose mansion that had been her home for much of her childhood. The sight of it stirred a strange mixture of emotions—resentment, sadness, and the faintest hint of nostalgia. She stepped out of the car, her heels clicking against the gravel driveway as she walked toward the front door.

Inside, the house was exactly as she remembered it—cold, imposing, and filled with the lingering scent of old wood and polished furniture. The housekeeper, an elderly woman named Mrs. Dalton, greeted her quietly, her eyes betraying the sadness she had undoubtedly felt in the wake of her employer's passing.

"Miss Pierce, welcome back," Mrs. Dalton said softly, her voice a far cry from the formality of the city world Amelia had left behind. "Your father would be proud of you, I'm sure."

Amelia gave a stiff smile, not knowing how to respond. Her father's approval had always come with strings attached, and she wasn't sure she wanted any part of it now. She was here only out of obligation, not because she wanted to honor his memory.

As Amelia wandered through the vast, empty rooms of the mansion, she felt as if she were walking through a ghostly version of her past. The grandeur of the house felt hollow now, devoid of the life it once held. She couldn't help but feel the weight of the decision before her, the enormity of the task she was now expected to undertake.

The ranch. Her father's legacy. It was all too much for her to handle. But she had no choice. Amelia knew she would have to face the ranch, take responsibility for the future of the estate, and make the hard decisions her father had left behind.

But as she looked out the window toward the rolling hills and the barns in the distance, Amelia couldn't help but feel that a part of her had already been lost to this place. And yet, there was no turning back.

The clock was ticking. And the ranch awaited her.

3

The Man in the Stables

The morning sun filtered through the towering oak trees that lined the edge of the estate, casting long shadows across the well-maintained grounds. Amelia Pierce stood in front of the stables, her heart pounding in her chest. The vastness of the ranch stretched out before her, both awe-inspiring and intimidating. She had known this place as a child, but now it felt like a world she didn't belong to. The ranch was nothing like the corporate world she had mastered—there was no sharp, cold precision here. It was all raw earth, wild grass, and the occasional distant sound of horses grazing in the fields.

She'd been told the horse trainer, Lucas Caldwell, was waiting for her inside the stables. Amelia's eyes flicked over the old wooden structure, the scent of hay and horses heavy in the air. There was a strange calm about the place, but beneath that calm was a quiet tension. A tension she couldn't place but could feel in her bones.

Taking a deep breath, she stepped inside, the heavy barn door creaking open as she walked through. The stables were lined with pristine stalls, each housing a horse that stood quietly, some with their heads out, others with their backs turned. But at the far end of the barn, standing at the edge of a large stall, was a man she hadn't yet met.

Lucas Caldwell.

He was leaning against the wooden fence, his arms crossed over his broad chest, watching one of the horses as it lazily moved about in its pen. He didn't look up as she entered, his posture relaxed but commanding. His clothes were simple—worn denim jeans, a faded flannel shirt, and heavy boots. His dark hair was tousled, and his face, though handsome, was hardened by years of living a life that was far from the polished world of high-rises and boardrooms.

Amelia cleared her throat, taking a step forward.

"Mr. Caldwell?" she called out, her voice echoing slightly in the quiet barn.

Lucas turned slowly, his expression unreadable. There was a flicker of something in his eyes—surprise, maybe, or irritation—but it was gone as quickly as it appeared. He didn't smile, didn't move to greet her. He simply studied her for a moment, his gaze cold and calculating. Amelia felt an unexpected chill run down her spine.

"You must be Miss Pierce," he said, his voice low and gravelly, like he'd spent years shouting commands to stubborn horses.

"Didn't think you'd be this soon."

Amelia wasn't sure how to respond to that. Was he surprised she had arrived, or was he just indifferent? It was hard to tell with him. She offered him a tight, polite smile, stepping further into the stable, trying to appear more at ease than she felt.

"I arrived early," she replied, her voice steady despite the butterflies in her stomach. "I'm here to go over the details of the ranch, and... to meet you."

Lucas studied her for a long moment, his gaze scanning her from head to toe. Amelia straightened, suddenly self-conscious. She had always prided herself on her professional demeanor, her ability to command attention in a room. But here, standing in front of a man who was clearly at ease in this world, she couldn't shake the feeling that she was out of place.

"Right." He nodded slowly, pushing himself off the fence and taking a few steps toward her. "So, you're the one inheriting this mess." His words were blunt, but not unkind. It was clear that he didn't mince words. Amelia's heart skipped a beat, but she forced herself to stand firm.

"I'm here to do what needs to be done," she said, her voice calm but firm. "I may not be familiar with ranching, but I can handle the responsibility."

Lucas chuckled under his breath, but there was no humor in it. "Handling responsibility is one thing. Understanding it is another."

The challenge in his voice was unmistakable. Amelia's temper flared slightly, but she knew better than to let it show. She had worked her way to the top in a male-dominated industry, and she had never let anyone push her around. She wasn't going to let Lucas Caldwell do it either, no matter how much he seemed to tower over her both physically and emotionally.

"I'm not here to argue," she replied coolly, stepping closer to him. "I'm here to learn. And I'd appreciate your cooperation."

Lucas finally looked her in the eye, the intensity of his gaze making her heart race. "Cooperation," he repeated slowly, as though testing the word. "You think you can just walk in here and take over? You don't know the first thing about ranching. This place isn't some corporate office you can manage with a few meetings and spreadsheets."

Amelia's jaw tightened, but she didn't back down. She had worked too hard to be underestimated, and she wasn't about to let a man—no matter how ruggedly handsome—make her feel small.

"I may not know the first thing about ranching, but I do know how to manage a business," she said, her voice steady. "I will figure it out. I'm not asking you to like it. I'm asking for your help."

There was a long pause as Lucas studied her. His expression softened ever so slightly, but it wasn't a smile. He just seemed to be taking her measure. Finally, he nodded, though it seemed like an unwilling concession.

"Fine. I'll help. But you'll need to learn quickly. Things aren't as simple as you think."

Amelia didn't know if that was meant to reassure her or challenge her, but she nodded. "I'm ready," she said, meeting his gaze.

For the first time, Lucas seemed to relax a little, a flicker of something like respect crossing his features. "Alright, then. Let's start with the horses. Follow me."

Amelia followed him as he led her to the far end of the barn. She wasn't sure what she expected, but what she saw surprised her. The horses were magnificent—strong, powerful creatures that seemed to embody the spirit of the ranch itself. Their coats gleamed in the light filtering through the windows, and their eyes were sharp and intelligent, sizing Amelia up just as Lucas had done.

"This one's Luna," Lucas said, gesturing toward a black mare with a white streak running down her forehead. "She's a handful, but she's loyal once she trusts you."

Amelia nodded, impressed by how easily Lucas moved among the animals. He wasn't just a horse trainer; he was a part of this world. He had a deep connection to these creatures, something that Amelia couldn't quite grasp but couldn't deny either. She felt like an outsider here, a woman who didn't belong in this realm of dirt, sweat, and horses.

But for some reason, the more time she spent with Lucas, the more she realized that maybe, just maybe, she could learn. She could learn to understand the rhythm of the land, to respect the animals that lived here. But most of all, she could learn to respect Lucas, a man who had been shaped by this land in ways she couldn't even begin to understand.

She glanced at him again as he gently stroked Luna's neck. There was something about the way he moved, the quiet strength in his demeanor, that both unsettled and intrigued her. He was not the man she had imagined when she first heard about him. Lucas Caldwell was not just a ranch hand or a trainer. He was something more, something that pulled at the deepest parts of her.

For the first time since she arrived at the ranch, Amelia felt a flicker of something she hadn't expected: curiosity. Maybe she wasn't as out of place here as she thought. Maybe this ranch, this life, held more than she could see. Maybe, just maybe, Lucas Caldwell was the key to understanding it all.

But as she watched him interact with the horses, a thought whispered at the edge of her mind—what if this world wasn't just about land and animals? What if there were things here, dark and complicated, that she wasn't ready to uncover?

4

Old Wounds and New Struggles

The morning sun was still low in the sky when Amelia walked across the sprawling ranch grounds, her boots crunching on the gravel driveway. The crisp air of the countryside filled her lungs, sharp and bracing, as if it was pushing away the lingering heaviness of city life. The estate stretched out in all directions, an expanse of land she had never fully appreciated until now. It was beautiful, yes, but with that beauty came an overwhelming sense of responsibility. Her father's death had thrown her into this world—this world that she had spent so many years trying to escape.

Amelia had always been someone who thrived on control—on decisions made in boardrooms, on strategies executed under tight deadlines, on legal jargon and contracts that left no room for error. But here, in the open fields of Pierce Ranch, there was no room for strategy. No room for control. No neatly tied-up legal documents that could solve her problems with a signature.

It was a world that required hands-on involvement, day in

and day out, dealing with dirt, animals, and unpredictable challenges. It terrified her.

She made her way to the stable, her thoughts swirling with everything she had been tasked with. Her father had always seen the ranch as a legacy—a place where tradition and business had merged. But to Amelia, it was just a place where she had once lost her mother and been suffocated by her father's overbearing presence. And now, it was hers to command. Or, so it seemed.

When she entered the stables, the scent of hay and leather hit her, familiar but foreign at the same time. The sound of horses shifting in their stalls filled the space, their quiet whinnies a stark contrast to the tension she felt within herself. She had been here for a few days now, trying to immerse herself in the rhythm of ranch life. But no matter how much she tried, there was always that feeling—an incessant reminder that she was not supposed to be here, that this place was never meant to be hers.

Lucas Caldwell stood at the far end of the stables, his back to her, working with one of the horses. She could see the muscles in his back flex as he moved with the animal, his movements calm, and confident, a perfect reflection of the way he was with the ranch itself. He didn't rush. He didn't force. He simply let things unfold as they would.

She hated him for that. Hated him for being so at ease with it all while she struggled to even know where to start.

Amelia stood at the entrance for a moment, watching him, her heart hammering in her chest. She had learned to bury her emotions, to keep her composure in every situation, but today, something about this place was different. The responsibility, the overwhelming weight of the ranch's future, was bearing down on her, and she could feel herself cracking under the pressure.

"Lucas," she called out, her voice sharp, cutting through the quiet hum of the stables.

He turned slowly, his gaze meeting hers with that same unreadable intensity she had seen every time their paths crossed. There was no smile, no welcome—only a steady look that made her feel like he could see straight through her.

"Miss Pierce," he said in that same gruff tone as if addressing a distant acquaintance rather than his employer. "I was expecting you."

"Amelia," she corrected quickly, though the formality still stung. She wasn't used to people not using her title, and she hated the reminder of it. The distance in his tone made her feel like an outsider in her own family's legacy. "I need to talk to you about the ranch."

Lucas took a step toward her, wiping his hands on a rag as he approached. "What about it?" His voice was casual, but there was a hint of wariness in his eyes.

"I've been thinking," Amelia began, her hands clenched at her sides. "The future of this ranch. We can't keep going the way it has been. My father's methods were outdated, and I'm not sure we can keep it running like this without some serious changes."

Lucas arched an eyebrow, clearly intrigued but cautious. He didn't speak immediately, just waited, letting her continue.

"We need to modernize. We need to diversify the income streams. I've been thinking of ways to integrate the land with more profitable ventures. Maybe something with tourism, farm-to-table dining, or even local events. The old ways aren't sustainable anymore," Amelia said, her voice gaining strength as she spoke, the words pouring out faster than she could control.

Lucas studied her for a long moment before responding, his gaze unwavering. "You think you can just come in here and turn this place into something it's not?"

Her chest tightened at his words, but she refused to let him see how much they stung. "This place is a business," she snapped, frustration bubbling to the surface. "And businesses evolve. My father didn't adapt to the changing world, and that's why the ranch is in the shape it's in now."

A long silence passed between them, and Amelia could feel the air between them thickening, heavy with unspoken words. Finally, Lucas spoke, his voice low and controlled.

"You think you can come in here and just change things without understanding the land, the people, the animals?" he asked, his tone hardening. "You're looking at this like it's just numbers and profit margins. But this ranch isn't a spreadsheet, Amelia. It's a living, breathing thing. You can't just force it to be something it's not."

Amelia's heart raced as she absorbed his words. The sharpness in his tone, the intensity in his eyes—it was as if she was speaking to a different person than the one who had been polite and quiet just days before. This was the side of Lucas she hadn't seen before—the one who cared about the ranch, about preserving its integrity. And he was right. She hadn't been thinking about the ranch as something more than a business. She had been thinking about it as a project, a thing to fix.

Her gaze softened slightly. "I know this isn't easy," she said quietly, her voice almost trembling. "But I have no other choice. This place is all I have left of my father, and if I don't make the changes needed, it could all disappear."

Lucas's expression softened for the briefest of moments, but then his jaw tightened again. "Your father didn't leave you this place to turn it into a tourist trap, Amelia. He left it to you to care for, to protect. And that means understanding it, respecting it."

Her frustration mounted again, and she stood taller. "I'm not trying to disrespect it," she said, her voice firm. "But if we don't change, it won't survive. I want to save this place, Lucas. But I can't do it alone."

Lucas's eyes held hers for a long moment. The tension between them was palpable as if they were both trying to push each other to the breaking point. Finally, he sighed, his shoulders slumping slightly as he gave in.

“Fine,” he said, his voice rough. “We’ll work together. But you’re going to have to prove that you’re not just here to run this place like a corporation. The land, the animals, the people who work here—they’re not just assets, Amelia. They’re part of what makes this ranch what it is. If you can understand that, then maybe we’ll get somewhere.”

Amelia stared at him for a long moment, the weight of his words sinking in. He wasn’t wrong. She had spent so much time trying to fix the ranch with her business mindset that she hadn’t stopped to understand what it truly meant. But she wasn’t ready to back down either.

“I’m ready to learn,” she said quietly. “But I need your help. And I need your trust.”

Lucas’s gaze remained hard for a moment before he nodded as if he was reluctantly accepting her terms.

“You’ll have my help,” he said, turning back toward the horses. “But trust is earned, not given. Let’s see if you can prove that you’re worth it.”

Amelia stood in the stables, watching him as he turned away, and for the first time since arriving at the ranch, she felt a glimmer of hope. She had a long road ahead, but maybe—just maybe—there was a way forward for both of them.

5

Uneasy Beginnings

The early morning fog still lingered over the ranch, wrapping the land in a quiet, dreamlike haze. Amelia stood near the stables, her boots sinking slightly into the damp earth beneath her feet, eyes scanning the ranch with an unfamiliar sense of responsibility. She had been back at the estate for over a week now, and each day brought more challenges than the last. It wasn't just about running the property—it was about learning a new language, understanding the rhythms of the land, and trying to fit herself into a role she never wanted. And yet, here she was, standing in front of a ranch that demanded her attention.

The crisis had come up quickly—one of the horses had fallen ill. Amelia had no idea what was going on, but it seemed serious. Lucas had been called to handle it, of course. He was the ranch's expert, the one who understood the horses better than anyone else. Still, that didn't mean she could just stand by and do nothing. This was her responsibility now, even if she felt woefully unprepared.

As she approached the stables, she could hear Lucas talking to someone—or something. Her heart skipped as she realized the voice was low and gentle, coaxing something—someone—into cooperation.

"Easy, boy," Lucas murmured, his voice calm but firm, with an undertone of command. "You're alright. We'll get you through this."

Amelia stepped inside, moving quietly so as not to disturb the scene unfolding before her. She paused for a moment, watching Lucas work. He was kneeling beside one of the larger stalls, his attention entirely focused on the horse. The animal, a massive brown gelding named Thunder, was visibly distressed, his sides heaving with shallow breaths. Lucas had a reassuring hand on the horse's neck, murmuring to him, his fingers brushing the animal's coat in slow, soothing motions.

The sight was unexpected. Amelia had assumed Lucas would be more commanding, more forceful with the situation. Instead, he was calm, almost reverent, as though he understood that sometimes, force wasn't the answer. He was gentle, yet unyielding in his focus.

She took a few cautious steps forward. "Is everything alright?" Her voice broke the tension in the air, and Lucas looked up sharply, his dark eyes meeting hers.

"Amelia," he said, his tone measured but carrying a slight edge of surprise. "I didn't expect you to be here."

"I didn't expect to be either," she said, her lips curling into a tight smile. She gestured to Thunder, the large horse still lying down in the stall. "What's going on?"

"It's colic," Lucas explained, his voice steady but tinged with concern. "The horse's digestive system is in trouble. We need to keep him calm, give him the right treatment before it gets worse." He stood slowly, his tall frame towering over her as he stepped away from the horse. "You should step back. I'm going to need space to work with him."

Amelia hesitated, feeling the weight of the situation settle in. Colic. It was one of the most serious conditions a horse could face, and it was clear that Lucas was concerned, even if he tried to hide it. She had no idea what she could do to help—she barely knew the first thing about horses.

"I can help," she said, more out of instinct than anything else. She wasn't sure why she said it, but there was a part of her that needed to prove herself, to show that she wasn't just a city girl trying to take charge of a world she knew nothing about.

Lucas raised an eyebrow, looking at her with a mix of disbelief and skepticism. "This isn't the time for you to play hero, Amelia. It's a delicate situation."

"I understand that," she snapped, feeling a sharp edge to her tone. She didn't like being dismissed, not when it came to something this serious. "I want to learn. You have to let me try."

For a moment, Lucas stared at her, the weight of his gaze heavy on her skin. Amelia held her breath, unsure of what would happen next. Finally, he exhaled slowly, his shoulders relaxing just a fraction.

"Alright. Do you want to help? Fine. But stay out of my way."

She nodded, relieved but still on edge. This wasn't how she had envisioned her first real task as the ranch's new caretaker. She had expected meetings, strategy sessions, and some sort of executive summary about the ranch's operations, not an emergency with a sick animal. But here she was, in the thick of it, feeling both terrified and determined to prove herself.

As Lucas moved back to Thunder, Amelia followed his instructions from a distance, watching him work. His hands were steady as he carefully administered medicine to the horse, his brow furrowed in concentration. The horse seemed to respond to him—he trusted Lucas, and Lucas trusted the animal in return.

"Do you want me to hold him?" Amelia asked tentatively after a few moments, as the horse seemed to shift uneasily. She wasn't sure why, but there was something in the way the horse looked at her—maybe it was the vulnerability in his eyes—that made her want to step in.

"No," Lucas said firmly. "He won't trust you yet. You're a stranger, and he's already stressed enough."

The words stung a little, but Amelia didn't let it show. She watched as Lucas continued working, a quiet intensity in his every movement. As the minutes ticked by, the tension in the air seemed to loosen, and Amelia couldn't help but be impressed by how easily Lucas commanded the situation. He wasn't just a man who worked with horses; he was someone who understood them, respected them, and had an uncanny ability to communicate with them in ways that Amelia could never have anticipated.

As the procedure progressed, Amelia felt a strange shift inside herself. She had always been a woman in control, always the one who could handle any situation with the power of her intellect, the force of her will. But here, in this barn, surrounded by the quiet power of nature, she felt small, helpless in the face of something she couldn't simply talk or negotiate her way out of. She wasn't the boss here. She was just another person in the world Lucas had mastered.

The silence in the barn was broken only by the occasional soft grunt from Thunder and the sound of Lucas's steady breathing. Amelia was struck by the calmness of the moment, the way Lucas seemed to have mastered the art of presence, of being. There was something magnetic about him—the way he held the space, the way his confidence bled into every action, every word.

Her thoughts began to wander, but she quickly shook them off. She had no time for distractions. Thunder's condition was still critical, and Amelia couldn't afford to lose focus.

"Is he going to be okay?" she asked, finally allowing the

question to escape her lips.

Lucas glanced up at her, his expression unreadable. "He's stable for now," he said quietly, wiping his hands on a rag. "But it's still touch and go. We'll know for sure once he's had time to rest and settle."

Amelia exhaled, feeling a wave of relief wash over her. She didn't realize how much she had been holding her breath until the weight of it lifted.

Lucas turned to her fully now, wiping the sweat from his forehead with the back of his hand. His eyes were softer now, not the hard, unapproachable look she had seen before.

"Thanks for your help," he said, his voice quieter than before. "I know you didn't have to stay."

Amelia smiled faintly, the warmth of the moment catching her off guard. "I'm starting to think I might learn a thing or two about ranching after all."

He nodded, the briefest of smiles tugging at the corner of his lips. "You might. Just don't expect it to be easy."

Amelia chuckled softly, feeling a strange sense of satisfaction wash over her. Maybe this was what she needed—more than just a corporate title or legal victories. Maybe she needed to prove to herself that she could be something more, that she could overcome the obstacles in her path. But just as quickly as the thought appeared, she pushed it aside. The future was still uncertain, and the ranch was still a daunting challenge. She couldn't let her emotions cloud her judgment.

But one thing was clear—working with Lucas Caldwell had already started to change her. And it was a change she couldn't ignore, no matter how hard she tried.

As the morning wore on and the crisis seemed to stabilize, Amelia found herself standing next to Lucas, watching as Thunder slowly regained his footing, the horse's deep brown eyes watching them both with a wary but grateful look. For the first time since arriving, Amelia felt like she had accomplished something here, and for a fleeting moment, she allowed herself to believe that maybe, just maybe, she could succeed at this ranching business.

But as she looked at Lucas out of the corner of her eye, she couldn't shake the feeling that the bond they had just shared was only the beginning. The beginning of something far more complicated. And she wasn't sure if that was a good thing.

6

The Memory of Home

Amelia stood in the doorway of the old mansion, the heavy scent of wood and aged leather filling her senses. The grand estate was far from the sleek, minimalist apartment in the city she had become accustomed to. Here, every piece of furniture, every framed painting, every corner seemed to carry the weight of generations. The high ceilings and intricate moldings spoke of wealth, but they also whispered of something long lost—a legacy, a life, a time she had once known and then fled.

As her eyes swept across the familiar yet alien space, memories rushed in like a tide she hadn't expected. The dining room table where her family had gathered for Sunday dinners—long since emptied. The staircase she used to rush down, a child with boundless energy, clutching her books as she chased after her dreams. Everything was the same, yet everything had changed. The house was just as she remembered it, but she was different.

She stepped into the hallway, her footsteps muffled by the thick carpet beneath her. The walls seemed to close in on her as she passed old family portraits—her father's stern face, her mother's soft smile, a younger version of herself frozen in time. She had run from this life, as far as her city ambitions could take her. She had traded the dusty, quiet streets of this town for the bustling cityscape where she could build her career, and carve out her identity away from the shadows of her family. Yet, here she was, back in the same house that once held so many painful memories. The house reminded her of the expectations, and the responsibilities she had always tried to escape.

Her father's death had thrown her back into this world, whether she liked it or not. The will had been clear: she was to take over the ranch. The same ranch her father had poured his soul into for decades. But Amelia wasn't sure if she had the strength, the will, or the desire to continue it. She wasn't a rancher and the business side of things felt like a cumbersome weight she was expected to carry without ever having learned the ropes.

With a deep breath, she walked further down the hall, her fingers trailing lightly over the wall as if trying to ground herself in the past. As a child, she had always loved this house, its vastness, its beauty. But it had also been a prison—a place where her father's expectations of her had suffocated her, where her mother's absence had left a void she could never fill.

Her parents had been distant, not in the way of neglect, but in the way of their preoccupations. Her father had been consumed with his ranching empire, obsessed with making Pierce Ranch one of the most successful in the area. Her mother, though loving, had always seemed overwhelmed by the weight of it all.

She had died when Amelia was still young, and in her absence, Amelia had been forced to grow up quickly, to fend for herself in a house that was always too large and too quiet. There had been no comforting words, no reassurances. Just silence and a need for perfection that Amelia had never quite been able to meet.

Her mind wandered back to the present as she approached her father's study—the room where decisions had been made, contracts signed, where the weight of the ranch had been felt most acutely. The door was ajar, and she could see the large mahogany desk, the leather chair, and the shelves lined with books, journals, and documents. Amelia hesitated before crossing the threshold, the familiar yet unfamiliar atmosphere of the room making her uneasy.

She stepped inside, her heels clicking sharply against the wooden floor, a stark contrast to the quiet stillness of the room. The desk was exactly as it had always been, cluttered with papers, an ashtray full of cigarette butts, the faint smell of old cigars lingering in the air. Her father's presence still felt strong here, as if he might walk in at any moment and resume his work. But there was no voice, no command, no forceful presence. Just the quiet of his absence.

Amelia moved to the desk, her fingers brushing over the papers. There were contracts, business proposals, bills—nothing new. She had expected to find something more, some clue as to what her father had planned for the ranch in his absence, but there was nothing. Only more of the same, endless responsibilities and decisions she didn't know how to make. She sighed, pushing the papers aside.

Her eyes landed on a framed photograph sitting on the edge of the desk. It was a picture of her mother, taken on a warm summer day. She was smiling, her brown hair falling loosely around her shoulders, her hands resting gently on Amelia's small shoulders. Amelia's younger self smiled back at her mother in the photo, a joyful, carefree expression on her face. It was a different time, a time before the weight of expectations had crushed her. Amelia's fingers hovered over the frame, but she didn't touch it. It felt too personal, too painful.

She turned away from the desk and walked toward the window, the weight of everything pressing down on her chest. Outside, the ranch stretched out into the distance, rolling hills dotted with grazing cattle and horses. The land was beautiful, but it felt like a different world, one that she had no place in. The city was calling to her, the world she knew—the world where she had made a name for herself, where she had control, where she was in charge.

But here, she was just Amelia Pierce, the daughter of a man who had never asked her what she wanted.

A soft knock at the door pulled her from her thoughts. She turned around, startled.

"Amelia?" Lucas's voice called out from the other side, quiet but firm. "Are you in there?"

She didn't respond immediately, unsure if she wanted to face him yet. There was still so much between them—the tension, the unspoken words. But she knew Lucas would wait. He always did.

She opened the door slowly, her gaze meeting his. He was standing in the hallway, his posture relaxed but his expression unreadable.

"Is everything alright?" Lucas asked, his eyes scanning the room behind her, taking in the quiet, the stillness.

Amelia nodded, forcing a small smile. "Just thinking."

Lucas didn't seem convinced. He stepped inside the room, looking around with a critical eye. "It's a lot to take in. The ranch. The family history. You're not here by choice, are you?"

Amelia's eyes flickered with uncertainty. She didn't know how to explain it. How could she? Even she didn't fully understand why she was still here, still trying to carry out her father's wishes when it felt like an impossible task.

"No," she admitted finally, her voice quiet. "I'm not here by choice. But... I don't have any other option." She met his gaze, her expression conflicted. "It's what I've been left with. The ranch. My father's legacy. I have to try. But I don't know if I can."

Lucas's eyes softened for a moment, his gaze growing more understanding. He stepped closer, his presence oddly reassuring. "You don't have to do this alone, Amelia. I'm here. We're here to help."

For the first time, Amelia felt something close to hope—a flicker of possibility. Maybe it wouldn't be so hard to navigate this world. Maybe she didn't have to do it on her own.

But as she looked out the window at the sprawling estate, she couldn't shake the feeling that no matter how much help she had, she was still trapped by the weight of her father's legacy. And that, more than anything, was what would determine the future of Pierce Ranch.

Amelia closed her eyes, the weight of the past and future pressing down on her shoulders. She had to decide, sooner or later, whether she could truly take the reins or whether the ranch would take her down.

7

Unexpected Help

Amelia sat at the kitchen table, staring at the pile of documents in front of her. The ranch's financial records were a mess, disorganized and incomplete. Her father's meticulous nature had left her with a mountain of paperwork, contracts, and pending deals, but no clear direction. She had expected things to be difficult, but she hadn't anticipated just how overwhelming it would feel to suddenly inherit this vast, sprawling estate.

The early morning light filtered through the large kitchen windows, illuminating the rustic charm of the room, but it did little to ease the tension in her chest. Her coffee cup was long forgotten, now cold and abandoned beside the papers. She ran her fingers over the top of the nearest contract, feeling the weight of it, the sense of responsibility that came with her name at the top.

"Are you planning to stare at that all day?"

Amelia jumped at the sound of Lucas's voice, her gaze snapping up. He stood in the doorway, arms crossed, his dark eyes fixed on her with an unreadable expression. There was no escaping him—not now, not after everything that had happened.

"I'm not sure what to do with it all," Amelia admitted, her voice tight. "There's so much to go through. I'm not sure where to start."

Lucas moved into the room, his boots clicking softly on the wooden floor. He walked over to the table, his gaze scanning the mess before him. It had been a week since they had dealt with Thunder's colic, and since then, things had only seemed to get worse. Amelia had been juggling the ranch's daily operations on her own, a task she'd never signed up for. Her hands were tied, and she couldn't shake the feeling that her father had known this would happen. She was being tested—pulled into a life she wasn't prepared for, and now the weight of it all was pressing down on her, crushing her under the expectations.

Lucas stood quietly beside her, taking in the situation. "You've been at this for hours," he remarked, his tone gentle but laced with something akin to concern. "Maybe it's time for a break."

Amelia shook her head, frustration evident on her face. "I can't afford a break. The bills are piling up, and there are contracts here that need to be signed by tomorrow. My father's business operations are in shambles. How could I let this happen?"

Lucas took a step closer, his presence almost overwhelming. "You didn't let it happen, Amelia. Your father didn't leave you a manual on how to run this place, and this kind of thing takes time. You're doing your best, and that's all anyone can ask for."

She stared at him, unsure whether she wanted to believe him. Part of her wanted to yell at him, to tell him that he didn't understand. He had his way of doing things, his way of running things, and that was the problem. Every time they worked together, there was tension between them. The walls between them were only growing higher, and yet he was still standing there, offering help, giving advice. He wasn't supposed to be her ally. He wasn't supposed to care.

"I don't even know where to start," she said quietly, exhaling a breath she didn't realize she had been holding.

Lucas, sensing her vulnerability, let the silence linger for a moment before speaking again. "Maybe we should start with something simple. You don't have to tackle everything at once."

She raised an eyebrow, skeptical. "And how do you suggest we do that?"

He sat down across from her, his face hardening slightly. "I know you don't want to hear this, but I'm offering to help. You've been carrying this burden by yourself for too long, and it's clear that you're struggling. I know the ranch. I know how it runs. Let me help."

Amelia blinked in surprise. She hadn't expected him to offer his help again, especially after their last interaction. The tension between them had only worsened, and his presence always felt like a storm waiting to break. She had spent most of her time avoiding him, keeping things professional, trying to make sure their paths didn't cross too often. The idea of working together made her stomach tighten.

"I don't need charity," she said, though her voice lacked the conviction she had hoped for.

Lucas didn't flinch at her words. "I'm not offering charity, Amelia. I'm offering help. You can't do this alone."

The raw honesty in his voice caught her off guard. She looked at him, really looked at him for the first time in days, and for the first time, she saw the seriousness in his expression. The lines around his eyes were more pronounced than they had been when she first met him, and there was a weight to his posture—like he had been carrying something for a long time, something he hadn't shared with her. There was no pretension, no bravado. It was simply the look of a man who was offering what he could, asking for nothing in return.

The silence between them stretched on for a long moment. Amelia could feel her resolve weakening, the tight grip she had on her independence loosening with every second. She had been trying so hard to hold it all together. She had convinced herself she didn't need anyone. But in that moment, looking at Lucas, she realized that maybe, just maybe, she did.

"What's the catch?" she asked, her voice low, betraying her cautious curiosity.

Lucas leaned forward slightly, the faintest trace of a smile tugging at his lips. "No catch. Just help. But you'll need to trust me. I can't help you if you don't trust me."

Sera let out a long breath, weighed down by the decision in front of her. Trust wasn't easy for her. Trusting someone had always been difficult—especially after what she had experienced in the city, where everyone seemed to have their hidden agenda. But here, in the quiet of the ranch, it felt different. And yet, a small voice in the back of her head warned her that Lucas, for all his charm and skill, might have his reasons for offering help.

But she was running out of options, and maybe, just maybe, this was the opportunity to make things right. To give the ranch a chance. To give herself a chance.

"I'll take your help," she said, the words feeling strange as they left her mouth.

Lucas's expression softened. "Good. But we'll do this on my terms. No shortcuts, no half-measures. You'll learn the ropes, and we'll do this right."

Amelia nodded, swallowing back the flood of emotions threatening to overwhelm her. She didn't know if she could do it, but with Lucas's help, maybe she had a shot. Maybe there was hope.

As they dove into the stacks of paperwork together, Amelia couldn't shake the feeling that the storm was far from over. Something still simmered beneath the surface, something she couldn't quite put her finger on. But for the first time in a long time, she wasn't alone in this fight. And for now, that was enough.

But in the back of her mind, a quiet question echoed: Was this partnership truly for the ranch, or was there something more that Lucas was after?

8

The Hidden Pain

Amelia stared out the window of the ranch's dining room, watching the sun dip below the horizon, casting a warm, amber glow over the rolling hills. The wind swept through the trees, rustling the leaves in a comforting whisper. It was a sight she had always taken for granted—one she had never thought to appreciate. But now, as she stood in the center of the grand old house, with its worn yet timeless elegance, she found herself grappling with more than just the responsibility her father's death had thrust upon her. She was also grappling with the realization that the life she had chosen—her city career, her escape—was nothing more than a fragile construct.

This estate, this ranch, was part of her blood, even if she had spent years running from it.

She turned from the window as she heard the sound of footsteps approaching. Lucas was coming from the stable, his boots leaving marks on the wooden floor as he walked. She hadn't expected him to show up tonight. In fact, after their recent tense moments, she had almost hoped he'd give her some space. But he hadn't.

"Couldn't sleep either?" Lucas asked, his voice low and smooth, just a little guarded. He was leaning against the doorframe, his strong arms crossed over his chest, eyes flickering to hers with a mix of curiosity and caution. The way he looked at her, as if always waiting for her next move, still unsettled her.

Amelia met his gaze but didn't answer right away. Instead, she glanced over the papers scattered across the table—business, contracts, and promises she didn't want to make. The ranch had grown too large, and the expectations too heavy. The land, her father's legacy, was slipping through her fingers. And, even with Lucas's help, it seemed like there was no way to keep it together.

"I didn't expect to see you tonight," she said quietly, trying to keep the annoyance out of her voice.

Lucas stepped further into the room, the muscles in his broad frame rippling with each step. "I figured you might need company." He gave her a slight, almost imperceptible grin. "You've been at this all day."

Amelia sighed, letting her shoulders drop. She didn't have the energy for another argument. "I don't think the company is going to solve anything."

Lucas's grin faded as he crossed to the table and sat down, taking a seat across from her. For a long moment, he said nothing, his gaze fixed on the papers before him. The silence stretched uncomfortably, but Amelia didn't mind. In truth, she was exhausted—physically, mentally, emotionally. She had spent so much time building her city career, making a name for herself, and now she was here, caught between a life she never wanted and a family legacy she never thought she'd return to.

Then Lucas spoke, breaking the silence. His voice was quieter now, more serious. "You know, I didn't want to be here either."

She looked up, startled. "What do you mean?"

He leaned back in his chair, his eyes wandering to the far corner of the room as if lost in thought. "When I was a kid, I wanted out of this place. I wanted to leave all of it behind." His words were heavy, his tone laced with a bitterness that made Amelia pause. "But life doesn't always give you a choice, does it?"

Amelia wasn't sure how to respond. She had always seen Lucas as someone who was in control, someone who had the ranch and the land figured out. He had a quiet strength about him, an air of someone who belonged here, who thrived in this environment. But this... this vulnerability was new.

Her heart tightened in her chest. "You never told me much about your past. You've been so focused on the ranch, on helping me..."

"I know," Lucas interrupted, his voice tinged with frustration. "But there's a lot you don't know about me, about my family. About why I'm still here, still trying to make this work."

She felt the weight of his words, his unspoken story, but she wasn't sure if she wanted to hear it. His life, his history, had been his own—his pain was his own, too. But something in the way he looked at her now, something softer, urged her to listen.

"Why don't you tell me, then?" she said cautiously, her voice barely above a whisper. "I'm listening."

He studied her for a long moment before finally nodding, as if deciding whether to trust her with the pieces of himself he had kept locked away. "My father was the ranch manager before me. The one who made it all work—before it all came crumbling down."

Amelia leaned forward slightly, her curiosity piqued. She had no idea what he was going to say, but something in his voice told her that it wasn't just about the land—it was about the man, about the struggle.

Lucas continued, his words slow and deliberate. "He was tough. Old school, you know? The kind of man who expected everything to be earned. There was no softness in him, no room for mistakes. And when I wanted to leave, to go to college, to make something of myself beyond this ranch, he told me I was weak." He clenched his jaw, his eyes darkening. "I didn't know it at the time, but he was right in his way. I wasn't ready to take on the weight of this place. I wasn't ready for responsibility. I wasn't ready to stay and fight for it."

Amelia's heart began to beat faster, her empathy overwhelming her as she watched him struggle to keep his emotions in check.

"What happened?" she asked softly.

"I left," Lucas said, his voice thick with regret. "I went to college, got my degree, and thought I could forget all of this." He gestured vaguely to the ranch, to the land that stretched out beyond the window. "But the thing is, you can't outrun your roots. And when my father passed away, there was no one left to keep this place running the way it should. No one else cared about it as much as I did. So, I came back." He paused, swallowing hard. "I came back to fix what I thought was broken. To make something good out of the wreckage."

The silence in the room was deafening, filled with the weight of his confession. Amelia felt a surge of sympathy and understanding for him, though she could see the deep scars his past had left on him. He wasn't the confident, unshakable man she had thought him to be. He was just as broken, just as scarred, as she felt inside.

"So you've been here all along," she said softly. "Fighting for this place, for something you don't even know if you want anymore."

Lucas nodded, his gaze finally meeting hers. "It's not just about the land, Amelia. It's about proving something to myself. It's about proving I'm not weak, that I'm not just some kid running from his problems. And it's about proving to everyone who thought I'd fail that I can make this place work again."

The sincerity in his words struck Amelia deeply. It was the kind of vulnerability she had never expected from him. It made her see him in a new light—not just the rugged, determined rancher, but a man who had been shaped by pain, by failure, by the weight of his past.

For a moment, they both sat there, lost in the silence, as if sharing this fragile truth between them had built an invisible bridge—a connection neither of them could deny.

Finally, Amelia spoke, her voice softer than she intended. "We're not so different, you and I."

Lucas raised an eyebrow, his lips twitching slightly. "How do you figure?"

She smiled faintly, the weight of the moment making her feel more vulnerable than she ever had before. "We're both here because we're trying to prove something. I've been running from my past for years, thinking I could leave it all behind. And now, here I am, back in the place I swore I'd never return to."

Lucas's expression softened as he studied her as if seeing her for the first time. "Maybe it's not so much about running away, Amelia. Maybe it's about facing what we've been avoiding for so long."

The words lingered between them, heavy with meaning. For the first time, Amelia felt like she understood Lucas in a way she never had before. He wasn't just the horse trainer, the man who had been here all along. He was a man carrying his burdens, just as she was.

And in that moment, she realized that maybe, just maybe, they could carry their burdens together.

9

Conflict at the Heart of the Ranch

Amelia stood at the edge of the ranch, looking out over the vast, rolling fields. The late afternoon sun bathed the land in a soft golden light, and for a moment, she felt at peace. The ranch, despite its worn fences and outdated equipment, held an undeniable beauty. It was a place of memories, both painful and precious, and she couldn't help but wonder how things had gotten so complicated.

She had thought she could handle the return to the family estate—after all, she had built her career with her own two hands. But here, among the ranch workers, the land, and the legacy of her father, Amelia felt like an outsider. And the community, with its long-standing ties to the Pierce family, was only making it harder.

The meeting earlier that day had been uncomfortable, to say the least. The workers, most of whom had known her father for decades, were not happy to see her in charge. They hadn't voiced their dissatisfaction directly, but it was clear in their tense faces and whispered words. It didn't help that she didn't know the first thing about running a ranch, let alone the history that was so deeply ingrained in this place.

"Amelia, you've been quiet," Lucas's voice broke through her thoughts. She turned to see him walking toward her, his usual confident stride interrupted by the solemnity that seemed to have settled between them.

"I'm not sure what to do with all of this," she said, motioning to the land that stretched endlessly before her. The ranch, once vibrant and alive with the promise of prosperity, now seemed to be weighed down by its history.

Lucas stopped beside her, glancing out over the land with an expression of deep contemplation. "It's not easy, I know." His voice was low, more thoughtful than usual. "You've got the workers—men and women who have worked this land for generations. And then there's the history of your family, all wrapped up in this place. They're not going to take kindly to changes, especially not from someone who's been away so long."

Amelia looked at him, her brow furrowing. "I know they don't like me being here. They don't trust me." Her voice trembled slightly as she spoke, betraying the frustration she felt.

Lucas sighed, glancing at the group of workers who were unloading hay bales from a truck nearby. "It's not personal. They've worked hard to keep this ranch running, and now, they see someone who doesn't know the first thing about it coming in and trying to change everything. It's going to take time for them to come around."

She nodded slowly, her mind racing. "But I can't just sit here and pretend things are fine the way they are. The ranch is falling apart. The buildings need repairs, the fences are breaking down, and the financial situation is worse than I thought. I have to do something."

"You're right," Lucas agreed. "But it's not just about what you want, Amelia. It's about what the ranch needs. And right now, it needs the community to work together, not to divide further." He gave her a pointed look. "You've got the people here who are willing to help, but you have to earn their trust first."

She swallowed hard. "I don't know if I have enough time for that."

Lucas was silent for a moment before speaking again. "You might not have time, but you've got heart. And that can go a long way." He paused, his gaze steady as it met hers. "But you need to understand that you're not just dealing with business and land here. You're dealing with history, with people who've given their lives to this place. It's not something you can fix overnight."

Amelia bit her lip, glancing back at the workers, who were now moving in their usual rhythm, their faces unreadable. She could feel the weight of their judgment pressing down on her, even from a distance.

"I don't know if I can do this, Lucas," she admitted, her voice barely above a whisper. "I don't have the knowledge. I don't know how to fix what's broken."

Lucas's eyes softened, and for a moment, he didn't say anything. He just stood there with her, watching the workers, and she could feel the quiet support in his presence. She wasn't sure if he fully understood what it felt like to be in her shoes, but in that moment, she appreciated his silence more than any words of encouragement he could offer.

"I'll help you," he said finally. "I know this place better than anyone. I can guide you, and teach you what you need to know. But you have to be patient. This place is built on trust, and if you push too hard, it could all fall apart."

Amelia felt a flicker of hope at his words. "You'd really help me?"

He nodded. "Of course. We've got a lot of work to do, but I think we can make it work. We'll start with the basics. We'll take it one step at a time."

Her heart softened at his offer. It wasn't just about the ranch anymore. Lucas's offer of help felt like a lifeline. In a world that seemed to be pulling her in different directions, he was the one constant she could rely on. And yet, part of her couldn't shake the fear that by relying on him, she was letting her guard down. There was still so much she didn't know about him, and his motives remained unclear.

Just as the moment began to settle, the sound of a truck engine roared to life, breaking the quiet. Amelia looked up, her eyes narrowing as she saw the truck driving down the dirt road toward them, kicking up dust in its wake.

"It's Bob," Lucas said, his voice low. "One of the ranch workers. He doesn't take kindly to changes. I think he's here to have a word with you."

Amelia straightened, a knot forming in her stomach. "I don't want any more confrontations."

"Get used to it," Lucas said, his tone gruff. "Bob's not one to let things slide. He's been here longer than most of the people working on this ranch. If you want to make this work, you'll have to face him."

The truck came to a halt in front of them, and Bob stepped out, his eyes hard and unreadable beneath the brim of his worn hat. He was a tall man, built like an oak tree, with a weathered face that showed years of hard labor.

"Amelia Pierce," he said with a nod, his voice thick with the local accent. "I didn't expect to see you back here."

She straightened, trying to hold her ground. "I didn't expect to be here, either," she replied, her tone calm, though her nerves were starting to show. "But it's where I need to be."

Bob's gaze flicked to Lucas, who stood beside her, his arms crossed. The tension in the air was palpable, and Amelia could feel the weight of the unspoken words between them. Lucas had never been on Bob's side, and Bob had never been a fan of Lucas's laid-back attitude toward the ranch.

"This ranch means something, Ms. Pierce," Bob said, his eyes narrowing. "It's not just a piece of property. It's a legacy. And you need to understand that before you start making decisions about its future."

Amelia swallowed. "I do understand, Bob. I just... I need to make changes. This ranch has been left in a bad state, and I'm here to fix it."

Bob didn't move, his gaze unwavering. "Fix it, huh? Well, that's the problem. We've been doing this for generations, and we don't need someone from the city coming in here telling us how it's done."

The words stung, but Amelia didn't flinch. She had expected this kind of hostility. What she hadn't expected was how much it affected her.

"I'm not here to tell anyone what to do," she said, her voice steady. "I'm here to help. But if you're not willing to work with me, we won't get anywhere."

Bob looked at her, his eyes calculating. For a moment, Amelia feared that he might turn away, dismissing her completely. But after a long pause, he spoke.

"We'll see what you're made of, Miss Pierce," he said, his tone begrudging. "If you're serious about this, you'll have to prove it to us. One step at a time."

As Bob walked back to his truck, Amelia felt the weight of his words settle in. She wasn't just fighting to save the ranch. She was fighting for respect, fighting to prove that she could stand on her own two feet and lead.

But as she stood there, with the sun sinking lower in the sky and the ranch stretching out before her, she realized that the road ahead would not be easy. She would have to prove herself to more than just the workers here—she would have to prove herself to herself.

10

A Glimpse of Vulnerability

Amelia stood in the middle of the ranch's central yard, the midday sun beating down on her shoulders, feeling heavier than usual. The air was thick with the scent of hay and earth, the smells of a life she was only beginning to understand. The workers were scattered across the grounds, some tending to the horses, others maintaining the fencing. All were focused on their work, but Amelia knew their eyes were still on her, judging her every move. She could feel their skepticism in the weight of their silence.

She wiped a hand across her forehead, brushing away a strand of hair that had fallen loose from her ponytail. It wasn't the first time she'd stood here, trying to figure out how to make things right. After the heated confrontation with Bob the day before, Amelia had spent the night wondering how to break the tension. She was still new to all this—still not quite able to wrap her head around the way things had been done here for generations, the stubborn pride of the people who had worked this land.

But she couldn't let them think she wasn't trying. The ranch was hers now—whether she liked it or not—and she had to make it work. She had to show them, and herself, that she could handle this responsibility.

"Need help?" Lucas's voice broke through her thoughts, calm and steady as always.

Amelia turned to find him leaning against a nearby fence, his arms crossed, watching her with that unreadable expression. She was still trying to figure him out. There was a quiet strength about him, a sense of knowing what needed to be done, but always with a guardedness that made it difficult to know where he stood with her.

"I think I'm good," she replied, forcing a smile she didn't quite feel. "Just... trying to figure out where to start."

Lucas took a step closer, his boots crunching softly in the gravel beneath them. "It's not easy, running a place like this," he said, his voice low but not unkind. "I know it's a lot to take on."

Amelia met his gaze, feeling an unexpected pull in her chest. It had been a few weeks since she'd arrived, and yet, she still couldn't seem to find her footing. Every day was a new challenge—trying to understand the ranch, the workers, and even herself. She had come here seeking peace, trying to escape the pressure of the city, but the weight of her father's legacy had followed her, pulling her deeper into a world she wasn't sure she could control.

"I'm not sure I can do this, Lucas," she admitted, her voice softening with the weight of her vulnerability. She hadn't planned on saying it out loud, but the words had escaped before she could stop them. "I've spent my whole life trying to build something in the city, and now I'm here, trying to fix something that's been around for decades... it feels like I'm failing already."

Lucas's expression softened, and for the first time, Amelia saw a flicker of something deeper in his eyes—something more than just the professional mask he wore every day.

"Hey," he said, stepping closer, his voice reassuring but firm. "You're not failing. You're learning. It takes time, and it takes patience. More than you might realize."

Amelia let out a long breath, closing her eyes for a moment, letting the breeze wash over her. She wanted to believe him. She wanted to trust that this place—this ranch—was where she was meant to be. But every time she tried to dig in, to take control, the resistance from the workers and the weight of her doubts dragged her back down.

"You don't understand," she murmured, more to herself than to him. "The pressure of everything. The city, my family's expectations, the success I've built—all of it. It was always about being the best, always about proving myself. And now... I don't even know what I'm doing here."

Lucas watched her for a long moment, his brow furrowing slightly as if he were trying to understand the complexity of her words. When he spoke again, his voice was softer, more personal. “I get it,” he said quietly. “I’ve been there. Running from something because it feels too big, too much to handle. But sometimes you have to face it head-on to see if it’s something you can carry.”

His words hit her harder than she expected. Amelia had never been one to open up, especially not about her vulnerabilities. She had always kept her emotions hidden, behind the sharp, controlled facade she had perfected in the city. But here, with Lucas, it felt different. His calm presence made it hard to keep the walls she had built around herself in place.

“Why do you stay here?” she asked suddenly, her curiosity getting the better of her. She hadn’t realized how much she wanted to know about him, to understand the motivations that drove him, until the question slipped from her lips.

Lucas glanced away for a moment, his jaw tightening as though he were deliberating how much to reveal. When he spoke, it was with a quiet intensity, as if the words weighed on him. “Because this is where I belong. This ranch is all I’ve ever known. I was raised here, learned everything I know from my father. When he passed, I came back to take over, because I had to. It wasn’t a choice, it was a responsibility.”

Amelia watched him, sensing a pain beneath his calm exterior. She could see how much this place meant to him, how deeply rooted he was in the land. It wasn’t just about the work; it was about family, legacy, and the burden of responsibility that had been passed down to him.

"Doesn't that ever get to you?" she asked softly. "The weight of it all? The pressure to live up to something that was never your choice?"

Lucas's eyes flicked back to hers, and for a moment, she saw the ghost of something—something raw and vulnerable—before it was masked again by the steely resolve she had come to know. "Sometimes. But you learn to live with it. It's just part of who I am."

The words hung in the air between them, heavy with unspoken understanding. Amelia felt a connection to him in that moment—a shared understanding of the burdens they each carried. They were both bound to something—whether it was family, legacy, or expectations—and it was becoming clear to her that Lucas understood the weight of it in a way she hadn't expected.

She took a deep breath, trying to steady her racing heart. "I don't know how to do this," she admitted, the confession finally slipping from her lips. "I don't know how to run a ranch. I'm not cut out for it. I'm a lawyer. I'm used to high-rise offices, not fields and stables. I don't know what my father expected of me."

Lucas studied her quietly, his gaze searching, then he stepped a little closer as if he were trying to bridge the space between them. His voice was low and steady. "Your father knew you weren't like him. He knew you had your path to follow. And maybe he did expect you to take over this place, but not because he thought you were just like him. He probably thought you could bring something new, something different to it."

Amelia swallowed, trying to digest his words. The thought that her father might have believed in her—that he thought she could do more than just follow in his footsteps—was both comforting and overwhelming. She had always thought that he saw her as a failure, a disappointment for leaving the ranch behind. But maybe, just maybe, she had misunderstood him all along.

"Maybe I've been running from the wrong things," she whispered, more to herself than to him. "Maybe I haven't been facing what I need to."

Lucas nodded, his expression thoughtful. "We all run from something, Amelia. The trick is figuring out what we're running to, and if it's worth the chase."

For a long moment, neither of them spoke. The weight of their conversation hung in the air, settling between them in a way that felt both heavy and liberating. Amelia wasn't sure where this conversation would lead, but for the first time since she had returned to the ranch, she felt like she was starting to understand.

She wasn't alone in this. She had someone by her side, even if she hadn't realized it until now.

"I don't know what the future holds for this place," she said quietly, meeting his gaze once more. "But I'm willing to try. For it. For me."

Lucas's eyes softened, and he gave her a small, almost imperceptible smile. "That's all anyone can do. Try."

As the sun dipped lower behind them, casting long shadows across the ranch, Amelia felt a sense of peace she hadn't known she was looking for. Maybe, just maybe, she wasn't so alone in this fight after all.

11

The Inherited Burden

The weight of her father's legacy seemed to press down on Amelia with every passing day. Every corner of the ranch whispered memories, reminders of the past that she could no longer ignore. What had once been a place of comfort, a family home filled with love and life, now felt like an anchor pulling her down into uncertainty. The ranch wasn't just her inheritance; it was a lifeline, and that lifeline was starting to snap under the pressure of debts, broken promises, and a looming financial collapse.

It had been a long week since she'd learned of the deep financial troubles her father had left behind. A week of sleepless nights, of poring over documents, spreadsheets, and old contracts she had never thought to look at. It had been a week of learning that her father, the man she had always seen as a pillar of strength, had made choices that might very well be the undoing of everything he'd built. And now, she was the one left to pick up the pieces.

Amelia leaned back in the worn leather chair in her father's old office, her eyes scanning the final page of a contract that she had found buried deep within the file drawer. The figures on the page danced before her, each number more ominous than the last. There was no mistaking it now. The ranch was in deep trouble—more than she had realized.

She had known about the debts, the unpaid bills, and the loans that had been taken out over the years, but this... This was different. The estate had been mortgaged to the hilt, with interest payments mounting and a deadline fast approaching. There was no way she could repay it all. Not on her own.

Her father had left her with a choice, but it wasn't one that felt like a gift. She could sell the land—the very land that had been in her family for generations—or face the reality of bankruptcy and losing everything. She could already feel the sting of the words on her tongue. The thought of selling this place, of giving it up to the highest bidder, was something she couldn't even begin to process. It wasn't just property to her—it was her past, her childhood, her father's legacy. But now, the ranch was slipping through her fingers like sand.

She slammed the papers down onto the desk, frustration burning in her chest. She had tried so hard to keep it together. She had tried to do everything her father had asked, to live up to his expectations, but in the end, she was left with nothing but a crumbling empire.

"Amelia?"

The voice startled her, and she looked up to see Lucas standing in the doorway, his face etched with concern. He hadn't knocked—he never did—but that wasn't what caught her attention. It was the way he was looking at her, like he knew something was wrong even before she had said a word.

"I didn't mean to interrupt," he said quietly, stepping into the room. His usual confidence was gone, replaced by something softer. He was always so composed, but today, there was an air of vulnerability about him that she couldn't ignore.

"No," Amelia muttered, trying to force a smile. "It's fine. I just—" She paused, glancing down at the papers in front of her. She didn't want him to see how close she was to losing control. "It's just a lot to handle."

Lucas didn't say anything for a long moment, simply standing there and waiting. He was patient in a way that always surprised her, as though he knew exactly when to push and when to let her be. Amelia hated that he could read her so easily, hated how he could see through her walls without even trying. But she couldn't bring herself to shut him out—not this time.

Finally, she spoke, her voice trembling. "There's no way around it, Lucas. The ranch... it's in debt, and it's been mortgaged. My father left me with nothing but a ticking clock."

She stood up abruptly, pacing around the room, her mind racing. The room felt too small, the walls closing in on her. Her breathing grew shallow as the weight of it all crushed down on her chest. She had come back to this place hoping to make things right, to find some kind of peace after everything that had happened, but instead, all she was finding was chaos.

"I have to sell it," she whispered to herself, though the words tasted bitter on her tongue.

The silence between them was deafening. Lucas had remained still, watching her with that same unreadable expression. His jaw was clenched, but there was no judgment in his eyes. He wasn't looking at her like she had failed. Instead, there was an understanding, an unspoken sympathy that made her heart ache.

"I'm not sure what else I can do," she continued, her voice cracking. "I don't have the skills to turn this around. The ranch was never meant to be my responsibility. I never wanted this, Lucas. I never asked for it."

Lucas stepped forward, his voice low but firm. "You don't have to do it alone, Amelia."

She looked at him, startled by the sincerity in his voice. "What do you mean?"

"I mean that I'm here," he said, taking a step closer. "I've been here for a long time. This ranch—it's my life, too. If you're going to make a decision about its future, you don't have to do it by yourself."

His words hung in the air, a promise wrapped in vulnerability. For the first time since arriving at the ranch, Amelia felt like she wasn't just fighting this battle alone. But that also meant she would have to lean on Lucas—something that scared her more than she cared to admit.

"What are you asking me?" Amelia's voice was barely a whisper, the question escaping before she could stop it.

"Let me help you," he said, his voice steady. "We can figure this out together. But selling the ranch—your father's legacy—won't solve anything. It'll just leave you with a hole that won't be filled."

Amelia stared at him, uncertainty swirling inside her. She wanted to believe him. She wanted to trust that there was a way out of this mess, a way to save the ranch, to save the legacy her father had left her. But the fear gnawed at her, the fear that trusting Lucas might mean losing herself in the process.

"I don't know if I can do this," she said finally, her voice barely audible. "I don't know if I'm strong enough."

Lucas reached out, his hand brushing against hers. It wasn't a grand gesture, but it was enough to send a shiver through her. "You are stronger than you think," he said softly. "And I'll be here to help you every step of the way."

The sincerity in his eyes was undeniable, and for a moment, Amelia felt something shift inside her. It was the tiniest glimmer of hope, a feeling she hadn't allowed herself to experience in a long time. Maybe she could do this, after all. Maybe with Lucas's help, she could turn things around.

But the question still lingered in her mind—could she trust him completely? And even if she did, was it enough to save the ranch, or would it cost her more than she was willing to pay?

As the sun dipped lower on the horizon, casting long shadows across the estate, Amelia knew one thing for sure: this was only the beginning of the battle. And whatever came next, she wasn't going to face it alone.

12

The Unraveling

The letter sat in front of Amelia, its crisp white envelope almost mocking her as she sat at her father's old desk. The sun had just begun to dip below the horizon, casting long shadows across the room. The ranch house, though beautiful in its solitude, had begun to feel like a cage. Each creak of the floorboards, each gust of wind rattling against the windows, seemed to whisper the same thing—time was running out.

She hesitated, her fingers tracing the edges of the envelope, the weight of the decision she was about to make pressing down on her chest. Inside that envelope was an offer from someone who could solve all of her problems. A real estate developer, offering a price that was too good to pass up. The money could erase the debts, give her the freedom to walk away, to escape from the suffocating responsibility that had been thrust upon her. It was the pragmatic choice. The safe choice.

But it wasn't what her father would have wanted.

Her father had poured his blood, sweat, and tears into this ranch, this estate, and the idea of selling it felt like a betrayal. His legacy was in the land—the horses, the cattle, the barns—everything he had worked so hard to build. He had trusted her, and believed that she could carry the weight of the family name, but now the burden was crushing her.

And yet, the other part of her—the part that had always lived in the city, surrounded by luxury, comfort, and the constant noise of success—saw the sense in selling. The land was too much. It was too vast, too difficult, too full of memories she wasn't ready to face.

"Why is this so hard?" she whispered to herself, gripping the letter in her hand and staring out the window.

Her thoughts were interrupted by a knock at the door. She turned quickly, startled, and saw Lucas standing in the doorway. His dark eyes were soft with concern, his usual confident posture tempered by a hint of unease. He had come by nearly every day to help with the ranch operations, his expertise invaluable, though she still couldn't shake the feeling that he was holding something back from her.

"Amelia," he said quietly, his voice steady but unsure. "We need to talk."

She stood up, her stomach twisting with the unspoken tension between them. "About what?" She glanced back down at the letter, the weight of it still hanging over her.

"About the offer," Lucas said, stepping into the room, his gaze following hers as she set the letter back down on the desk. "I've heard rumors. Some of the ranchers are talking about it."

Amelia nodded, not surprised. Word spread quickly in a town like this, and the offer had stirred the waters. People had mixed feelings about the land being sold, though none of them seemed to understand what it meant for her.

"Have you made a decision?" Lucas asked, his voice low, almost hesitant.

"I don't know what to do, Lucas," she admitted, the words tumbling out of her before she could stop them. "Part of me wants to sell it. Get out, and start fresh. Let go of all the pressure, the debt, the constant struggle. It seems like the logical thing to do."

Lucas was quiet for a moment, his eyes studying her carefully as if weighing her words. He seemed to understand that it wasn't just about money—it was about something deeper. The legacy of her father, the inheritance that had been placed on her shoulders. The heavy burden of a ranch she had never really wanted but could not bear to lose.

"But the other part of me..." Amelia's voice faltered as she turned back to the letter. "The other part of me doesn't want to give up on this. It feels like giving up on everything I've ever known. Everything my father worked for."

She took a deep breath, her chest tight as the emotions that had been swirling inside her began to break free. "I don't know if I'm strong enough to make this work. I don't even know if I can. But I feel like if I sell it, I'm failing him. Failing myself."

Lucas took a step closer, his presence filling the room. He reached out and placed a hand on her shoulder, the touch both comforting and grounding. "You're not failing anyone," he said softly. "You're doing what you can. And whatever you decide, I'll be here."

For a moment, there was silence. The weight of his words settled between them, unspoken yet profound. Amelia could feel his support, his presence—something she had desperately needed since stepping back into this world.

But as much as his words were comforting, the decision still loomed large. She turned back to the letter, running her fingers over the neatly typed text, the promise of a fresh start staring back at her. The offer was tempting, a way out of the spiral of debt and responsibility that had taken over her life.

"But what if it's not just about the money?" Amelia said quietly, her voice barely above a whisper. "What if it's about something deeper? What if there's something here that I'm supposed to find, something that I'm supposed to do?"

Lucas didn't answer right away, as if he were carefully considering her words. When he finally spoke, it was with quiet sincerity. "This ranch is more than just property to you. It's a piece of who you are, Amelia. Your father's legacy, your family's history—it's all here. I can see how much it means to you, even if you don't want to admit it."

Amelia felt her chest tighten at the mention of her father. She had spent so much time trying to escape his shadow, trying to outrun the weight of his expectations, but Lucas was right. It wasn't just a building or a plot of land. It was part of her, whether she wanted it to be or not.

"I don't know how to keep it," she admitted, her voice cracking. "I don't know how to save it, to fix it. It feels like the walls are closing in on me."

Lucas's expression softened, and he moved to stand beside her, his presence a comforting reassurance. "You don't have to fix everything on your own. But if you want to fight for this place—if you want to save it—then you're going to need help. And you've got it. From me."

For a long moment, Amelia didn't know what to say. Her thoughts were still swirling, torn between practicality and emotion, between the desire to escape and the pull of her father's legacy.

She wanted to believe that she could do this. She wanted to believe that she could find a way to save the ranch, to bring it back to life. But the weight of it all, the responsibility, the looming deadline—everything seemed too much.

But then she remembered something her father had always told her: "You don't give up. Not when things get tough. You fight for what you believe in."

She had spent so many years running from the ranch, from her past, but maybe it was time to face it. Time to stop pretending that she wasn't capable of more than she thought.

Amelia squared her shoulders and turned toward Lucas, her eyes meeting his with newfound resolve. "I won't sell it," she said firmly, her voice strong despite the uncertainty that still lingered in her heart. "I'm going to fight for it. For this place. For my father."

Lucas nodded, his eyes filled with a quiet admiration. "Then I'll help you. We'll figure it out, together."

And just like that, Amelia made a decision. She was no longer running. The ranch, her father's legacy, her future—they were all in her hands now. The path ahead was uncertain, but for the first time in a long while, Amelia felt the weight of the world shift. And, perhaps, for the first time, she knew she wasn't alone.

As the last rays of the sun dipped below the horizon, Amelia knew one thing for certain: this was just the beginning of the battle to save everything that had once been hers. And with Lucas by her side, she felt ready to face whatever came next.

13

Secrets in the Barn

The air was thick with dust and the scent of old hay as Amelia stepped into the barn. The barn had always been a place of solace for her growing up—where her father had spent long hours working on the estate, where she had learned to ride horses, and where she and her father had shared some of their few quiet moments. But today, it felt like something else entirely. A place of secrets. A place of things left unsaid.

Her father's death had left a void that seemed impossible to fill. The family estate was too large, too full of memories for her to navigate alone. She had expected challenges—running a business she hadn't asked for, dealing with the financial instability—but what she hadn't prepared for were the things she was discovering in the wake of his death. The truth about her father, the secrets he'd kept, and the tangled web he'd woven to keep the ranch alive were all beginning to unfold, piece by piece.

She had come to the barn to clear her mind, to escape the weight of her responsibilities for a brief moment. But now, standing in the dim light of the barn, it felt like she had come to the edge of a precipice. Everything was about to change.

The small office in the corner of the barn was where her father had worked late into the night, going over accounts, dealing with the ranch's business dealings. It was also where he had hidden most of the things he didn't want anyone to know. The desk was covered in old papers, leather-bound books, and random notes. She had been through it all before, trying to get a better understanding of what had been left to her, what she had inherited.

But something was different today. As Amelia went through the stacks of papers again, a manila envelope tucked away in the back corner of the drawer caught her eye. It was hidden beneath a pile of receipts, its contents sealed with a single piece of tape. She couldn't remember having seen it before. It wasn't like the usual documents her father had kept—a few neat papers here and there, the odd contract or business agreement—but this... this was something else. Something that felt important.

Her heart skipped a beat as she lifted it, feeling the weight of it in her hand. She hesitated for a moment, fingers trembling ever so slightly. A nagging feeling crept over her that perhaps she wasn't meant to see whatever was inside. But the need for answers, the endless questions that had plagued her since her father's death, drove her to pry.

The tape came off easily, and inside the envelope, Amelia found several neatly folded sheets of paper. They were full of numbers—figures, sums, amounts. It took her a moment to realize what they were: financial statements. But these weren't the kind of reports she'd seen before—these were different. They were more personal, more detailed, and much darker than anything she'd ever seen on her father's desk.

Her mind raced as she scanned through the pages. The figures, the loans, the debts—they were all stacked against her father's estate. He had borrowed money from multiple sources—many of them illegal, many with questionable terms—and the debts had been mounting for years. It was worse than she had thought. He had put the ranch at risk, taking out loans he could never repay, and made deals that could cost her everything.

As the weight of the revelations settled on her, Amelia's breath quickened. This wasn't just bad financial planning—it was reckless, and dangerous. And now, it was her problem.

Her mind flashed to Lucas. He had warned her about the financial troubles, about the risks the ranch was facing. He had always been upfront with her, even when she hadn't wanted to hear it. But now she realized the full extent of it. How much of the estate was already spoken for, and how much of it was tied to debts that were past due? Her father had tried to keep the ranch alive by whatever means necessary, but it had all been a façade, built on shaky ground.

Amelia's stomach twisted as she read through the final pages. The last document, dated just a month before her father's death, was a letter—a letter she had never seen before. It was addressed to a man she didn't recognize. The tone of the letter was cold, and businesslike. But as she read it, the reality of her father's situation hit her with a brutal force.

The letter spoke of an agreement to sell the ranch if the debts couldn't be cleared within a year. It wasn't an option—it was a condition. If the terms weren't met, the land would be sold, and the estate would be taken from her. But worse still, her father had signed it, had agreed to the terms, perhaps without telling her. The estate was already slipping through her fingers, and she hadn't even realized it.

She sat back in the chair, her body numb, as the shock set in. The ranch—the legacy her father had built, the family history embedded in every inch of the land—was about to be lost. She had been left with nothing but a web of deceit, financial ruin, and a future she wasn't prepared to face.

The anger rose within her, a surge of emotion she couldn't control. How could her father have done this? How could he have placed everything they held dear on the line like this, without telling her? She felt betrayed, devastated, and alone.

Her mind flickered to Lucas. He had been right all along. She hadn't wanted to admit it, but the truth was undeniable now. He had seen the signs before she did. He had understood the risk and the danger, even when she had dismissed it. He had known about the debts, about the shady deals. But why hadn't he told her everything? Why hadn't he warned her more?

Frustration surged inside her as she balled the papers in her hands, the weight of her father's mistakes and secrets threatening to suffocate her. She had wanted so badly to fix things, to save the ranch and the legacy he had built, but now it felt like the pieces were falling apart faster than she could put them together.

She stood up, pacing around the room, her heart racing as she tried to think of a way out. But there were no easy answers. No quick fixes. She couldn't sell the land—it was too late for that. She couldn't pay off the debts on her own, not without risking everything. There was no escape, no way to undo the damage her father had done.

And yet, as she stood there in the silence of the barn, something else gnawed at her. Something deeper. It wasn't just the debts that haunted her—it was the sense of betrayal, the weight of the decisions she would have to make. She was stuck with a legacy she never asked for, and the more she uncovered, the more the burden of it all crushed down on her.

As she stepped out of the barn, Amelia's mind raced, her thoughts spiraling. The truth was out now. But the questions were still there—what would she do with it? What could she do? And, most terrifying of all, would she be able to save the ranch, or had she already lost it all?

Her father's secrets had come to light, but the future of the estate was anything but certain. The unraveling had only just begun.

14

A Test of Trust

The dark clouds had gathered on the horizon for hours, heavy and oppressive, but Amelia hadn't expected the storm to hit so soon. By the time the first gust of wind howled through the trees surrounding the estate, she knew they were in for something serious.

The ranch had always been subject to sudden weather changes—years of experience had taught her that, despite being in the city for so long. Still, nothing could prepare her for what she saw as she stepped onto the front porch. The wind picked up, howling, causing the trees to sway ominously, their branches creaking under the force. Amelia's heart began to race as the first droplets of rain fell, the skies darkening in rapid succession.

She had just started to call for the ranch hands when the wind whipped through the estate with terrifying speed. The gusts pushed past her with almost violent energy, carrying with them the unmistakable scent of rain and something else—something heavier, more foreboding. The storm was coming fast, and there was nothing they could do to stop it.

Amelia hurried toward the barn, her boots sinking into the wet earth as she moved. She had to check on the horses, the livestock, and the stability of the outbuildings. The last thing she wanted was for the animals to be left unprotected in the storm. She knew she couldn't do it alone—not with the damage that could come from winds this fierce.

As she approached the barn, she saw him—Lucas, already at the stables, leading the horses inside. His dark figure cut a striking silhouette against the darkening sky. There was no hesitation in his movements, no sign of panic. The way he moved—calm, collected, efficient—gave Amelia a sense of reassurance, despite the chaos around them.

"Lucas!" she called, her voice rising above the wind. He looked up at her, his expression unreadable. His dark hair was wet, clinging to his forehead, and his face was set with an intensity that matched the storm around them.

"Amelia," he said, his voice firm yet soft, as though everything was under control. "We need to get the barn doors secured. There's a good chance that the winds will pick up even more, and if those doors aren't shut properly, we'll have trouble keeping everything contained."

Amelia nodded, the sharpness of his gaze and the calmness in his tone pushing through the panic that had begun to rise inside her. She rushed to his side, helping him with the barn doors. The sound of the storm crashing around them was deafening, but in the midst of it, they worked in synchronized silence, each of them knowing exactly what needed to be done.

"I'll check the back and make sure nothing's damaged there," Amelia said, stepping back as Lucas finished securing the last door.

"Don't try to do too much alone," he warned, his hand resting on her arm for a moment, holding her in place. The touch sent a jolt of electricity through her, but she didn't pull away. Not this time. "We'll go together."

With a brief nod, Amelia followed Lucas toward the rear of the barn, where the wind was ripping through the trees like a freight train. The rain had turned into a downpour, thick sheets of water hammering the ground, creating deep puddles in the dirt.

As they moved toward the back of the property, Lucas pointed out areas of concern—loose fences, hay bales that had been knocked over by the wind, and, most urgently, the roof of the old horse shelter. Amelia could see it now—the edges of the roof lifting, threatening to fly off with the next gust of wind. The structure was on the verge of collapse, and if they didn't act fast, it would take the shelter down with it.

"Help me with the ropes," Lucas called, pulling some thick, weather-resistant rope from the back of the barn. He tossed one end to her, his hands working efficiently to tie the other around the posts of the shelter. The wind made it almost impossible to hear anything over the howl of the storm, but their movements were synchronized, practiced—almost as though they had done this before.

As they worked together, Amelia couldn't help but notice how close they were—his body moving beside hers in rhythm, his muscles taut as he strained against the storm. There was a connection between them now that hadn't been there before. Trust, built from the shared struggle of survival, from the urgency of the situation. The chemistry between them was undeniable, but neither of them said a word. It was an unspoken understanding, one that neither of them could ignore.

Once the shelter was secured as best as they could manage, they made their way back to the main house. The storm raged on, and with each step, the world around them felt smaller, more isolated. Amelia's heart was still racing—not just from the adrenaline of the work, but from something else entirely. The storm had forced them into a place where their personal barriers were slipping, where the lines between them were becoming harder to define.

As they reached the front porch, Lucas paused, glancing over at her. His expression was softer than it had been before, a subtle change that Amelia couldn't ignore.

"You did well," he said, his voice low, carrying a warmth that made Amelia's pulse quicken. "We make a good team."

Amelia's breath caught in her throat, and for a moment, she felt a pang of something she wasn't ready to admit. She opened her mouth to respond, but the words didn't come. The storm had stripped away more than just the roof of the barn—it had peeled back a layer of her, exposing emotions she'd spent months trying to keep hidden.

Lucas stepped closer, just a fraction of an inch, but enough to close the space between them. Amelia felt the weight of his presence, the intensity of his gaze, and the pull that had always been there—something magnetic, something impossible to ignore. For a moment, they stood in silence, the storm still howling around them, neither of them moving, neither of them speaking.

It was Lucas who broke the silence. "We should get inside. Before the roof comes down on us, too."

Amelia nodded, her pulse still racing, and turned to go inside. But as she stepped across the threshold, she felt his hand on her arm once more, his touch light but firm. She stopped, meeting his gaze, her heart hammering in her chest.

"You know," Lucas said quietly, his voice soft against the roar of the storm, "if you ever need help... if you ever need someone to lean on— "

She looked up at him, her breath shallow, her thoughts a whirlwind. She wanted to say something, anything, to acknowledge the emotions swirling between them, but the words caught in her throat. Instead, she simply nodded and entered the house, trying to calm the storm inside her.

Lucas followed her, and as they closed the door behind them, the storm continued to rage outside, but inside, something had shifted. Amelia could feel it—she had been tested, and she had come through stronger, with a new understanding of herself, and of Lucas. But what did it mean for them, moving forward?

The tension between them was no longer just about the ranch, or the work, or the storm. It was personal now. And Amelia wasn't sure if she was ready to face what it all meant.

But there was one thing she knew for certain: the storm may have passed outside, but inside, it was only just beginning.

15

The Tension Builds

Amelia stood by the wide windows, the ranch sprawling before her, bathed in the golden hues of the setting sun. The distant hills, familiar and unchanging, were comforting in their constancy, but as her gaze wandered across the land, a heavy knot tightened in her chest. The weight of responsibility was sinking in, and no matter how much she loved the idea of preserving her father's legacy, the reality was too daunting to ignore.

She had tried—really tried—to hold it together, to keep everything in line, to protect the ranch from the crushing burden of debt her father had left behind. But the offers from developers were starting to look less like a temptation and more like a lifeline. She needed to make decisions, hard decisions, to secure the future of the estate. And while part of her knew that selling could be the only way out, the other part—the part that had spent countless days in these fields as a child, the part that still believed in her father's dream—refused to give in.

Her thoughts were interrupted when the front door slammed

shut with a loud thud, causing her to flinch. She turned sharply, finding Lucas standing in the doorway, his expression hard as stone. His dark hair was disheveled from the wind, and his eyes burned with a mixture of frustration and something deeper—something she couldn't quite place.

"Amelia," he said, his voice low but laced with an edge she hadn't heard before. "We need to talk."

Amelia's stomach tightened, and she braced herself. She had been expecting this moment. It had been building for days, ever since she had gotten that final, unsettling offer from the real estate developers. She knew Lucas would be furious when he found out.

"You want to talk?" she asked, her voice a little sharper than she intended. "About what?"

He stepped further into the room, his boots heavy against the hardwood floor. "Don't play coy with me," he snapped, his voice rising. "You're planning on selling the ranch, aren't you?"

Amelia's heart skipped a beat. Her throat tightened, but she forced herself to stand tall. "I haven't made any decisions yet, Lucas. But if this ranch is going to survive, change has to happen. We can't keep going the way we've been going, pretending that it's all going to magically fix itself."

Lucas clenched his jaw, a muscle twitching in his temple. He was tense—too tense. She could see the anger simmering beneath the surface, but there was something else there, too. Something darker, deeper.

"You're talking about selling, Amelia," he growled. "You're going to sell out. You think just because you've got some fancy offers from developers, that you can walk away from everything this land stands for?" He took a step toward her, his eyes never leaving hers. "This land, my land, doesn't just belong to your father's legacy. It belongs to us. To me, to the people who've worked it for generations. And you think you can just hand it over to the highest bidder?"

Amelia's pulse quickened. She could feel the heat in his words, the anger, but beneath it was something else—something raw and painful. "It's not that simple," she said, her voice softening, though her emotions were anything but calm. "The ranch is drowning in debt, Lucas. The offer I received could save us—save everything. It's not about selling out; it's about survival. If I don't do something now, we might not have a ranch left to fight for."

Lucas's lips curled into a bitter smile. "Is that what you're telling yourself? That it's all just business? I thought you cared about this place, about the people here, about what we've all built. But clearly, it's all just about numbers to you. Isn't it?"

The accusation stung, and Amelia felt the familiar weight of frustration build in her chest. "That's not fair, Lucas," she said, her voice shaking with a mixture of hurt and anger. "I'm doing what's best. I didn't ask for this. I didn't ask for this responsibility. But I'm doing everything I can to keep it together."

His expression hardened, the anger in his eyes intensifying. "So you'll destroy everything we've fought for, just to make your life easier?" He took another step closer, and this time, Amelia didn't step back. She wasn't afraid of him—not physically, at least. But the words—his words—they felt like a punch to the gut.

"You think I want to sell? You think I want to lose this place?" Her voice rose, and she took a step toward him, not backing down. "But it's my decision now, Lucas. Not yours. My father made sure of that. And if I have to sell to make sure this ranch survives, then so be it."

Lucas's face reddened with frustration, his hands curling into fists at his sides. "You're not thinking this through. You can't just walk away from something like this. You can't just throw it all away because it's hard. If you sell now, you'll regret it for the rest of your life. Do you think you can live with that?"

Amelia froze, the weight of his words hitting her like a tidal wave. She was already regretting it. Regretting that she hadn't come back sooner. Regretting that she didn't have a solution. Her mind raced, torn between the desire to protect the land she had once loved and the need to escape the crushing responsibility.

"I'm not throwing it away, Lucas!" she snapped, her voice trembling. "I'm trying to save it! I'm trying to make sure it doesn't disappear completely. You don't get to tell me what's best for this place, not after everything you've kept from me."

The words fell between them like a heavy stone. For a moment, neither of them spoke. The tension in the room was palpable, thick, and suffocating. Amelia could hear the sound of her heartbeat, the rush of blood in her ears. She had never felt so exposed, so vulnerable. Everything she had tried to do in the last few weeks—everything she had worked for—was unraveling before her eyes.

Lucas took a deep breath, his expression softening for just a moment. "I don't want to see you make the same mistakes. I don't want to see you regret this."

Amelia's breath caught in her throat. She could hear the sincerity in his voice, but there was also something else—something deeper, darker. She was standing at the edge of a precipice, and she could feel the weight of the decision pressing down on her.

She wanted to believe in the future of the ranch, to believe in herself, to believe in the possibility of saving what her father had worked for. But the truth was, she didn't know if it was possible anymore. Her emotions were tangled, the threads too knotted to untangle.

"I'm doing what I think is right," she said, her voice quieter now. "But maybe it's not enough."

Lucas stood still, watching her, his expression unreadable. After a long silence, he spoke again, his voice much softer than before.

"I didn't want to see you walk away from it," he said, his tone almost gentle now. "But I can't make you stay. I can't make you change your mind. But whatever you decide, Amelia... just know that I'm here. And I'll fight for this ranch as long as I can."

His words hung in the air, as heavy as the storm clouds gathering outside. Amelia swallowed, looking away, unable to meet his gaze.

The battle for the ranch was more than just about land and money. It was about her—her place here, her future, her choice. And no matter how hard she tried to avoid it, the truth was becoming clearer with every passing moment: she was caught between two forces she didn't understand—her heart and her duty.

Amelia didn't know how the storm would end. But she knew, in that moment, the stakes had never been higher.

16

Crossing the Line

Amelia stood in the center of the estate's vast, open kitchen, her arms crossed tightly over her chest. The soft hum of the refrigerator was the only sound in the otherwise silent room, but it felt like an eerie stillness that suffocated her. Outside the large kitchen windows, the winds had picked up again, the tall trees swaying ominously in the distance, much like her thoughts. The storm that had been brewing all afternoon had now reached its peak, and it seemed to mirror the turmoil inside her.

She could feel the tension in the air, a weight that had been building between her and Lucas for days. But tonight, it had all come to a head.

Her gaze flickered toward the doorway, where Lucas had just stormed in, his expression dark and unreadable. His jaw was clenched tightly, his fists balled at his sides as if he were struggling to keep his emotions in check. The rawness in his eyes made her hesitate for a moment, a flicker of guilt pricking at her heart. But she couldn't let it distract her. The argument they had been having for weeks had escalated far beyond what she had expected. The lines between business and personal had blurred in ways that neither of them could ignore anymore.

"I don't get it, Amelia," Lucas said, his voice a low growl, his frustration clear. "You've been here for weeks, and all you've done is try to change everything my family and I built. The land, the ranch, the way things have been run... It's all been fine. Until you walked in with your city ideas. Now you want to sell everything off, like it's just a piece of property, a commodity to be discarded. What happened to the woman who loved this place?"

Amelia felt a sharp sting in her chest, but she held her ground. She wasn't going to let him make her feel guilty for doing what was necessary. She had her reasons, and they were valid. The ranch was on the brink of collapse, and every day spent pretending it could run without intervention was another day wasted.

"Nothing's fine, Lucas," she said, her voice shaking with controlled anger. "The ranch is drowning. I'm not some fool who can sit around and pretend that this is still the future my father envisioned. He didn't leave us with enough to carry it forward, and you know it as well as I do. Selling is the only way to save it."

Lucas's face hardened, the muscles in his jaw twitching with the tension building inside him. He took a step toward her, closing the distance between them, but she didn't retreat. Instead, she squared her shoulders, preparing herself for what was to come.

“Save it?” Lucas repeated, his voice a harsh whisper. “Save it by selling out to the highest bidder? That’s what you’re willing to do? Sell off the legacy, the land—everything that matters just to make some quick money?”

Amelia’s heart raced, her fists tightening at her sides. His words stung, but they weren’t fair. He didn’t understand, and it was becoming harder to explain.

“This isn’t about money, Lucas!” she snapped, her patience starting to wear thin. “You think I want to sell? I don’t. But I’m not going to sit around and watch everything fall apart because of pride. Your family doesn’t own this place anymore. It’s mine now. I have the power to make the decisions, not you.”

The silence that followed her words was deafening. The room seemed to shrink as the weight of her declaration hung in the air. For a moment, neither of them moved. Lucas’s face was unreadable, his fists still clenched tightly. His chest heaved with shallow breaths, and his eyes narrowed as if he were struggling to contain something dark beneath the surface.

“I don’t think you really understand what you’re saying, Amelia,” Lucas said, his tone cold now, almost threatening. “You think you can just waltz in here, tear everything down, and walk away with a neat little check at the end of it all? This place means more than that to me. It’s not just land. It’s not a business. It’s my family. It’s my home.”

Amelia's breath caught in her throat. His words cut deeper than she expected, the raw emotion in his voice making her question everything. She had always known that Lucas was passionate about the ranch, but hearing him speak about it like this—like it was his and not hers—made something inside her shift.

Her eyes softened as she studied him. She had never seen him this vulnerable before, never seen him this unguarded. But that didn't change the reality of the situation. She had to do what was necessary, even if it meant facing him down.

"Lucas," she said, her voice trembling slightly now, "I didn't come here to take anything away from you. But you're not seeing the bigger picture. This place is dying. And if I don't sell, it will disappear altogether. You have to let go of the past, of your attachment to it, and see it for what it really is."

Lucas's eyes darkened, his mouth set in a thin line. "You think I'm attached to the past?" he spat, taking another step forward. "You think I'm the one who can't let go? You know nothing about me, Amelia. Nothing about the work we've put in, the blood, sweat, and tears that went into making this place what it is. And you have the audacity to come in here and tell me it's all for nothing?"

The rage in his voice was unmistakable, and for a fleeting moment, Amelia wondered if he would lash out at her physically. His towering presence seemed to take up the entire room, his anger so palpable it made her feel like she couldn't breathe.

But instead of stepping back, she met his gaze head-on. She

wasn't afraid. She refused to back down.

"You don't get it," Amelia said, her voice steady but firm. "This isn't about pride. It's about survival. And if you want to save this place, you have to let go of the way it was. I'm trying to help you, Lucas. I'm trying to do what's right."

"Help me?" He laughed, the sound bitter and bitter. "I don't need your help. I need you to leave. To stop messing things up. This is not a game to me, Amelia. You think this is all just a business deal. But it's my life. And I can't just let you destroy it."

Amelia stepped back, the weight of his words sinking in. She couldn't believe what he was saying. She had spent so much time trying to do what was best for everyone, and this was the thanks she got?

"I'm not trying to destroy it," she said softly, her voice breaking. "But I can't just let it fall apart either."

The tension between them thickened. The air felt heavy, charged with emotions neither of them could fully control. They were both caught in a web of their own making, too proud to back down, too angry to forgive.

"Then maybe it's time we stopped pretending," Lucas murmured, his voice low and dangerous. "Maybe it's time we faced the truth of this situation. Neither of us is getting what we want. And if you think you can keep pushing me, you're going to lose more than just the ranch."

Amelia froze, her pulse quickening as the weight of his words crashed over her. What was he implying? And could she really afford to lose everything?

"I'm not pushing you," she said, her voice barely above a whisper. "But I will do whatever it takes to save this place."

Lucas's eyes flickered with something between anger and frustration, and in that moment, Amelia wasn't sure where they stood. She wasn't sure what was left to fight for.

The silence stretched between them, heavy, laden with everything unsaid.

"I'll do what I can," Lucas said, his voice thick with an emotion she couldn't decipher. "But you need to understand... we both have a lot more to lose than we think."

As he turned to leave, Amelia was left standing in the middle of the room, feeling more alone than ever before.

17

The First Kiss

The weight of the day hung heavily in the air, thick with unspoken words and unresolved emotions. Amelia stood at the edge of the porch, watching as the last remnants of daylight faded into twilight. The orange hues of the sunset had long since vanished, leaving behind a soft, muted darkness that settled over the ranch. It was peaceful here, away from the chaos of the city, yet the silence felt like a constant reminder of the storm brewing inside her.

She had tried to focus on the tasks at hand—the estate, the ranch's future, the growing tensions between her and Lucas—but all she could think about was the sharp, biting argument they'd had earlier that day. The words they had exchanged, the raw frustration in his voice, the way he had stormed out of the room, leaving her standing there, breathless and unsure. She had never imagined that managing her father's legacy would be so difficult, so painful.

And then there was Lucas. She had never meant for things to get so complicated between them. At first, it was just a professional relationship, two people thrown together by circumstances. But as the days wore on, it became something else. Something more dangerous. Every glance, every heated conversation, every shared moment of vulnerability—it all felt like a slow burn, simmering beneath the surface, ready to ignite at any moment.

As if on cue, she heard the creak of the door behind her. She didn't need to turn around to know who it was. The unmistakable sound of Lucas's boots on the wooden floor told her everything she needed to know.

"You've been avoiding me," his voice was low, rough with the remnants of their earlier argument. She didn't respond immediately, her eyes still fixed on the horizon. She wasn't sure what to say to him anymore, or even if she wanted to.

"Amelia," he said, stepping closer, his presence filling the space behind her. "I know things have been tense between us lately, but you can't just shut me out."

She finally turned to face him, feeling the tension crackle between them like electricity in the air. His expression was a mix of frustration and something else—something softer, more vulnerable. For the first time, she saw the weight he carried, the burden of his feelings. The anger was still there, but so was something else.

"I'm not shutting you out, Lucas," she replied quietly, her voice barely above a whisper. "I just... I don't know what to do anymore. This place, everything it represents—it's too much. And the way we've been pushing against each other, it's tearing me apart."

Lucas's gaze softened, and he took a step closer, closing the distance between them. She could feel the heat radiating off his body, the intensity in his eyes. Her breath caught in her throat as he reached out, his hand brushing lightly against hers, a gentle touch that seemed to hold all the weight of the emotions they had both been holding back.

"I know it's been hard," he said softly, his voice low and intimate, "but we can't keep fighting like this, Amelia. We can't keep pretending that we don't care about each other. I know you feel it, too."

Her heart raced in her chest, and for a brief, fleeting moment, she allowed herself to admit the truth. She did feel it. The attraction, the pull between them—it was undeniable. But it was more than that. It was a connection that ran deeper than anything she had ever experienced. And yet, there was a part of her that resisted, that couldn't give in to the desire coursing through her veins. She couldn't allow herself to be vulnerable, not when the stakes were so high.

"I don't know what to do, Lucas," she murmured, her voice trembling with the weight of her emotions. "I don't know how to fix this—us."

Lucas stepped even closer, his hand gently cupping her cheek, his touch warm and soothing. "You don't have to fix anything,

Amelia. We don't have to have all the answers right now. We just need to be honest with each other. We've been dancing around this for too long."

Before she could respond, he leaned in slowly, his lips hovering just inches from hers. The anticipation hung thick in the air, and for a moment, Amelia thought her heart might stop beating entirely. She could feel the heat of his breath on her skin, the magnetic pull that had been growing stronger with each passing day.

And then, without another word, Lucas closed the gap between them, his lips crashing against hers in a kiss that was everything and nothing like she had imagined. It was raw and desperate, filled with months of tension and longing. It was a kiss that demanded everything from her, a kiss that took her by surprise but also made her want more.

Her body responded instinctively, her hands finding their way to his chest, pressing against him as if she couldn't get close enough. She could taste the frustration, the desire, the hunger that had built up between them. For a brief moment, the world outside ceased to exist. All that mattered was the heat of his body against hers, the way his hands roamed, pulling her closer, deeper.

But just as quickly as the kiss had begun, Amelia pulled away, her breath ragged as she stared into his eyes. Her heart was pounding in her chest, her mind racing with confusion.

"No," she whispered, shaking her head. "I can't. We can't do this."

Lucas's brow furrowed, his expression one of confusion and hurt. "Amelia, don't pull away now. I know you feel it too."

"I do," she admitted, her voice barely above a whisper, her chest tightening with the weight of her emotions. "But we can't—we can't—do this. Not like this. Not when everything is already falling apart."

Her words hung in the air between them like an impenetrable wall. Lucas stared at her, his hands still on her arms, his touch gentle but firm. She could see the struggle in his eyes, the desire to push further, to take what was right in front of him. But she wasn't ready. She couldn't be.

"We can't keep doing this dance," he said softly, his voice a mixture of longing and frustration. "We can't keep pretending like there's nothing between us when it's all I can think about. But I get it, Amelia. I understand."

Sera pulled away from him slowly, her chest aching with the weight of everything unspoken. "I'm not saying I don't want this," she whispered, her voice strained. "But I'm not ready to lose myself in you. Not when I still don't know who I am without the ranch."

The words left her lips like a confession, a truth she wasn't entirely ready to face. But it was the truth. She had spent so long running from everything—her father's legacy, her past, the responsibilities that weighed on her shoulders—that she had forgotten who she was without all of it. And now, with Lucas, she was afraid to find out.

Lucas nodded slowly, his hands falling to his sides as he stepped back. He didn't say anything, but the look in his eyes told her everything she needed to know. He was hurting, but he was letting her go. For now.

"I'm not going anywhere, Amelia," he finally said, his voice soft but full of resolve. "But I'll give you the space you need."

Amelia nodded, a tear slipping down her cheek before she could stop it. She turned away, not trusting herself to say anything more. The kiss had been everything she wanted, and yet it had only made her more uncertain. She had crossed a line, and she wasn't sure if she could ever uncross it.

The question lingered in the air as she walked away from him: Could they go back to the way things were? Or had the kiss changed everything between them forever?

18

Rebuilding Bridges

The days that followed their kiss had been nothing short of agonizing for both Amelia and Lucas. The air between them had thickened with the weight of unspoken words and emotions they weren't yet ready to confront. Amelia, despite her resolve to keep things professional, felt a constant pull to Lucas—a tug at her heartstrings she couldn't ignore. The ranch, too, seemed to demand her attention, but the growing distance between her and Lucas made everything feel heavier.

She had avoided him for days, retreating into the comfort of her office at the estate, where the work was endless and, for a while, provided the perfect distraction. But even there, she couldn't shake the image of his face, the pain in his eyes, as he stood in the quiet of the night, giving her the space she so desperately wanted.

She had wanted to be strong. She had wanted to push him away. But deep down, she knew that if they were going to move forward—not just in their relationship, but in saving the ranch—they had to confront everything.

It was early one morning when the call came. Lucas wanted to meet.

She stood at the edge of the estate's expansive balcony, looking out over the land her father had left her. The cool breeze stirred her hair, and for a moment, it felt like she was standing on the precipice of something she couldn't control. The weight of responsibility pressed down on her like a physical force, and her mind raced with the possibilities—could she save the ranch? Could she even fix her relationship with Lucas?

She had no answers. Not yet.

But when the knock on her office door came a few minutes later, Amelia straightened, steeling herself. She opened the door to find Lucas standing there, his usual confident demeanor softened by an unspoken vulnerability. He looked at her, and for a brief moment, neither of them said anything. They simply stood there, facing each other, unsure of how to proceed.

"You wanted to talk?" Amelia finally broke the silence, her voice steady, though her heart hammered in her chest.

"I did," Lucas said quietly. "Can we sit?"

Amelia stepped aside to let him in, her eyes lingering on him for just a moment longer than she intended. There was something about the way he stood—solid, grounded, yet still slightly hesitant—that made her heartache. She had spent so many years running away from everything that connected her to the ranch, to her family, to him. But here he was, asking for a second chance, not just to salvage their relationship, but also to salvage the estate they both cared about so much.

They sat down across from each other, the table between them acting as a subtle barrier neither of them was willing to cross. For a few moments, there was silence again—this time, filled with the weight of everything they hadn't said to each other.

Amelia opened her mouth to speak, but Lucas beat her to it.

"I want to apologize," he said, his voice low, but filled with sincerity. "For everything. For pushing you too hard, for making this about me when I should've been more patient. I know I've been a bit... intense, but I'm not trying to control you. I want to work with you, Amelia. Not against you."

The vulnerability in his voice caught her off guard. For a long time, she had seen Lucas as this confident, almost indestructible figure, someone who had everything figured out. But now, sitting here, she realized just how much he had been holding back—the weight of his fears, his wounds.

"I've been running, too," she admitted softly, her eyes meeting his. "I've been running from this place, from you, from what I feel. But the truth is, I don't know how to face this without you. And I don't know how to fix things, Lucas. I'm not sure I even have the skills to do it."

Lucas reached across the table, his hand hovering for a moment before he gently touched hers, a silent acknowledgment of their shared struggles. Amelia's breath caught, but she didn't pull away. This time, the connection between them felt different—tangible, real, and fragile.

"We don't have to have it all figured out today," Lucas said, his voice soft. "But we have to start somewhere. We can't keep ignoring what's between us, Amelia. We both know there's something here. Something we can't just walk away from."

Amelia's heart skipped a beat. She had spent so much time avoiding what she felt for Lucas, but sitting here, feeling the warmth of his touch, she realized that she could no longer deny it.

"I'm scared," she admitted, her voice trembling slightly. "I'm scared of failing. Scared of the ranch falling apart. Scared of what it means if we don't get this right. And I'm scared of letting you in. Because if I let you in, it means trusting you—and trusting myself."

Lucas's hand tightened around hers. "I understand. I'm scared, too. But I want to be here. With you. Whatever this is, whatever we are, we'll figure it out together. You're not alone in this, Amelia."

She swallowed, her emotions threatening to overwhelm her. For so long, she had been running, both from the ranch and him. But now, sitting in front of him, she realized that running was no longer an option.

"What if we fail?" she asked quietly.

"Then we'll fail together," Lucas said with a small smile, his thumb gently brushing across her knuckles. "But at least we'll know we tried. Together."

The silence between them was heavy but comforting. Amelia could feel the walls she had built around her slowly beginning to crumble. It wasn't going to be easy, and it wasn't going to be perfect, but for the first time in a long while, she felt like she was ready to face what lay ahead.

"We'll try," Amelia said, her voice steady now, her resolve firming. "We'll try together."

For the first time in what felt like forever, Amelia felt a glimmer of hope. She wasn't sure what the future held, but she knew one thing for certain: she wasn't going to face it alone. Not anymore.

They stood up together, and as Lucas placed his hand gently on her shoulder, Amelia felt a sense of reassurance. It wasn't just about saving the ranch anymore—it was about rebuilding something far more important: their trust in each other, their shared commitment, and the bond they were beginning to build.

"Let's get to work," Lucas said, his voice strong and steady. "We've got a lot to fix, and we'll do it together. Starting with this place."

Amelia nodded, her heart lighter than it had been in days. She didn't have all the answers, and the road ahead would be anything but smooth. But with Lucas by her side, she finally felt ready to rebuild, not just the ranch, but everything they had left to salvage.

And this time, she wasn't running anymore.

19

The Pressure Grows

Amelia paced the length of the grand estate's living room, her hands clenched into fists as she stared out the window at the sprawling land her father had left her. The view, once peaceful and comforting, now felt like a prison—an inescapable weight pressing on her shoulders. The land was beautiful, but it was also a burden. Every day that passed, the pressure mounted, and with every passing moment, the threat of losing it all loomed closer.

She had spent her life building her career, establishing herself as a respected lawyer in the city, climbing the corporate ladder with a ferocity that had earned her a name. But here, in the heart of her family's estate, she felt more lost than she had ever been. The business associates in the city, the ones she had once trusted, were growing impatient with her reluctance to sell. They didn't understand the emotional ties she had to the land, the memories of her father, or the legacy she was trying to protect. All they saw was a piece of property—a piece that could be sold for a handsome profit.

And yet, as she stared out at the land, Amelia realized that Lucas was right. The ranch was barely holding on. The debts were piling up, the estate was in disrepair, and the workers—while loyal—were struggling to keep things running. She had come here to escape, to find solace, but she was only finding more and more reasons to doubt her ability to manage it all.

She had received the call earlier that day from her business associates, urging her to make a decision—soon. Their patience was running out, and they weren't going to wait forever. Amelia's eyes hardened as the words echoed in her mind. "Either you sell, or we'll decide for you. It's time to face reality."

She couldn't do it. She couldn't sell her father's legacy, no matter how many times they told her it was the only option. But the weight of their pressure was suffocating her, and deep down, she knew the ranch's future was at stake.

Just as her thoughts spiraled, she heard a soft knock on the door. She didn't need to turn to know who it was. Lucas had been a constant presence in her life these past few weeks, helping her navigate the difficult decisions and offering his expertise in ways she never expected. Despite their differences, they had become a team—albeit an imperfect one. But now, with the walls closing in around her, she felt her resolve faltering.

"Amelia?" Lucas's voice came from the other side of the door, his tone softer than usual.

"Come in," she called, turning to face him, the tension in her shoulders still present.

Lucas stepped into the room, his eyes immediately searching hers. He could always tell when something was bothering her, even when she tried to hide it. He took a step toward her, pausing when he saw the look on her face.

"Talk to me," he said, his voice steady but concerned.

Amelia shook her head, a wry smile forming on her lips. "I don't even know where to start."

"You're still thinking about the sale, aren't you?"

The question hit her like a punch to the gut. She nodded slowly, her fingers still tight on the edge of the table. "They're pushing me, Lucas. I'm not stupid. I know it's not just about the land anymore. It's about everything I've worked for... my career, my future. And every part of me is telling me to sell. To just let go and move on. But when I look at this place... when I think about what it means..." She trailed off, unable to finish the thought. She knew Lucas understood. They both knew the stakes were higher than she had ever imagined.

Lucas stepped closer, his presence calming but resolute. "Amelia, I know it's hard, but selling the land isn't going to solve everything. It might give you a short-term fix, but it's not going to take away the bigger picture. You've been running from the ranch for so long because it represents everything you've lost. But that doesn't mean it's not worth fighting for."

Amelia's eyes softened as she looked at him, but the doubt remained. "What if fighting for it means losing everything else? What if I end up losing myself in the process?"

Lucas sighed, reaching for her hand, his grip firm but gentle. "What if the only way to find yourself is by facing this? We've both been running, Amelia. I've been running from my past, and you've been running from your future. But this"—he gestured to the ranch—"this is where it all started. This is where the answers lie."

She wanted to believe him. She wanted to believe that they could fight for the ranch together, that they could build something real, something lasting. But the weight of the offer from her business associates still hung over her like a dark cloud.

"I'm so close to making a decision, Lucas," she said, her voice trembling slightly. "I'm not sure what's the right choice anymore. Sell and walk away, or fight and risk everything. But if I sell, I lose my connection to my father, to everything he worked for. If I fight, I risk losing my future."

Lucas's expression softened, and for a moment, he just looked at her as if he were seeing her for the first time—not as the businesswoman who had come back to manage the ranch, but as the woman who was carrying the weight of so much more than she could bear.

"You're not alone in this," he said, his voice low and reassuring. "Whatever you decide, I'll be here. You don't have to do it alone."

Amelia felt a lump form in her throat as the weight of his words hit her. She had spent so long fighting alone, afraid to lean on anyone, but here he was, offering her his support without hesitation. For the first time in a long while, Amelia felt like she wasn't carrying the weight of the world by herself.

She exhaled deeply, finally allowing herself to take a moment to breathe. "I don't know what the right choice is, Lucas. I really don't. But I think... I think I need to take a step back, to think about what I want. Not just for the ranch, but for myself."

Lucas nodded, his hand still resting on hers. "And I'll be here, no matter what you decide."

As Amelia looked at him, something in her heart shifted. The pressure that had been suffocating her felt a little lighter. She didn't have all the answers, but for the first time, she didn't feel like she was fighting this battle alone.

And as she looked out the window again, toward the vast ranch land stretching before her, she realized something. The decision she had to make wasn't just about the land, or about the future of her father's estate. It was about her. Her life. Her choice.

She didn't know what the future held, but she finally felt ready to face it.

With Lucas by her side, maybe it wouldn't be so impossible after all.

20

Confessions of the Heart

The sun was beginning to dip below the horizon, casting long shadows across the ranch. Amelia stood on the back porch, gazing out at the sprawling land that her father had once tended with such care. The land, which had always been her inheritance, now felt foreign, almost like a stranger's property. The weight of the decision that loomed ahead pressed on her chest, suffocating her.

She wasn't just deciding the fate of the ranch; she was deciding the course of her own life. And the more she thought about it, the harder it became to imagine a future that didn't involve the ranch in some way. But could she really bring herself to save it? Could she risk everything she had worked for in the city to preserve something that felt like a burden?

Her thoughts were interrupted by the sound of footsteps behind her. She turned to see Lucas walking up the porch steps, his expression unreadable, but his presence somehow comforting. They hadn't spoken much since their last conversation, and the tension between them was palpable. But now, as he stopped in front of her, their eyes met, and there was something unspoken hanging in the air between them.

"I've been thinking about what you said," Lucas began, his voice low, almost tentative. "About the ranch, about us."

Amelia swallowed hard, unsure of where this conversation was going. She had been holding back, afraid of the direction their relationship might take. She had always kept her emotions in check, especially when it came to matters of the heart. But there was something in Lucas's eyes, a vulnerability she hadn't seen before, that made her want to listen. She nodded silently, encouraging him to continue.

"I've spent my whole life here," Lucas continued, his voice thick with emotion. "My family's ties to this land run deep. But it wasn't until you came back that I realized... that I realized I'd always been tied to more than just the land."

Amelia's heart skipped a beat. She had always known that Lucas cared about the ranch, but she hadn't realized just how much. There had always been an intensity to his connection to the estate, a devotion that bordered on obsession. But what he said next made her stop in her tracks.

"I've loved this place," Lucas said, his eyes searching hers, "but I think I've also always loved you. I just didn't know it. Not until you came back."

The words hit Amelia like a jolt of electricity, her breath

catching in her throat. She stared at Lucas, trying to process what he had just said. For so long, she had kept herself emotionally distant, afraid to get too close, too involved. She had spent her life building walls, convinced that relationships were distractions. But in that moment, standing on the porch with Lucas, the walls began to crack.

"I don't know what to say," Amelia replied, her voice barely above a whisper. "I never expected... I never thought you'd feel that way. I came back here to escape everything I left behind. I didn't think anyone, especially you, would ever understand."

Lucas took a step closer, his hand reaching out to gently touch her arm. "I understand more than you think. I've spent so many years thinking I was alone in my love for this place, but the truth is, it was never just about the land. It was always about what it represented—what it means. It's the foundation of who I am. And you... you're a part of that now, whether you realize it or not."

Amelia's chest tightened as she tried to process his words. She had never allowed herself to believe in love, or in the possibility of belonging somewhere. She had always seen herself as an outsider, never quite fitting in with the people around her, always feeling like she was chasing something she couldn't define. But Lucas, standing there, with his unspoken words and the sincerity in his eyes, was making her question everything.

"I don't know if I can do this," she said quietly, her voice cracking. "I don't know if I can stay here, in this life. I've been running for so long, trying to build something in the city, trying to find my place. But now it feels like I've come back to something I didn't want."

Lucas's expression softened, his hand moving to cup her face gently. "I know it's hard. You've always been in control of your life, of your future. But this place... it's part of you, whether you want it to be or not. And I'm here. You're not alone in this."

Amelia closed her eyes, allowing his touch to calm her, to ease the storm of emotions swirling inside her. She wanted to push him away, wanted to walk back into the safe world she had built in the city, where she knew the rules. But here, with him, with the ranch, it felt different. It felt real.

"I'm scared, Lucas," she admitted, her voice trembling. "I'm scared that I'll fail. Scared that I'll lose everything, including you."

Lucas's thumb brushed against her cheek as he gently tilted her head back so she could look into his eyes. "You won't lose me. I'm not going anywhere. You're not alone in this fight, Amelia. We'll figure it out together. No matter what happens with the ranch, no matter what you decide, I'm here."

The sincerity in his voice, the way he held her gaze, made her heart ache with a longing she hadn't known she had. She had spent so much time building walls, convincing herself that love and vulnerability were weaknesses. But standing here, in this moment, with Lucas, she realized how wrong she had been. Maybe love wasn't something to fear—it was something to be embraced.

"I don't know if I'm strong enough for this," she whispered, her eyes never leaving his.

"You don't have to be strong alone," Lucas replied, his voice steady. "We'll be strong together."

For a long moment, they stood there, just the two of them, surrounded by the weight of the past and the uncertainty of the future. Amelia's heart raced, her mind swirling with questions and doubts. But for the first time, she felt like she wasn't alone in the fight. And in that quiet moment, she realized that maybe, just maybe, she didn't have to fight at all.

With a soft sigh, Amelia took a step forward, closing the distance between them. Her hand reached out to touch his, and when their fingers intertwined, it felt like the start of something new. Something real.

"I'm ready," she said, her voice steady but full of emotion. "I'm ready to fight for this. For the ranch. For us."

Lucas smiled, his grip on her hand tightening. "Then let's do it. Together."

As they stood there, side by side, the weight of the world no longer seemed so heavy. There would still be challenges ahead, still moments of doubt, but for the first time in a long while, Amelia felt like she had found a place where she truly belonged.

And that place—was right here, with Lucas, on the ranch that had once seemed like a burden, but was now a part of her future.

21

The Last Offer

The late afternoon sun cast a golden glow over the vast estate, but Amelia barely noticed the beauty around her. She sat in her father's old study, the weight of the decision ahead pressing down on her like a thousand-pound stone. The offer on the table was the final one—the developer, a man known for buying up prime real estate and transforming it into luxury resorts, had made it clear: Sell or he would take legal action to force a sale.

Amelia leaned forward, staring at the offer letter in front of her. It was tempting. She could walk away from the ranch and its mounting debts, leaving behind a life of responsibility and uncertainty. The money was more than she could ever need, and it would solve her problems—at least for a while. She could use the fortune to build a new future, free of the emotional baggage of her family's estate.

But as she read through the contract, the same nagging thought crept into her mind: what would she be giving up? The ranch had been her father's legacy. Despite all the difficulties and the unresolved issues that had haunted her family, the land was a part of who she was. And then there was Lucas.

Amelia looked up, her eyes wandering out the window toward the stables. She could almost hear the sound of horses galloping across the fields, their hooves thundering through the quiet countryside. Lucas had become more than just an ally in the past few weeks. His passion for the land was infectious. He had taught her so much about the estate, its history, and its potential. His belief in the ranch's future had given her hope when she had felt ready to give up.

But now, with the developer's offer staring her in the face, she couldn't help but feel torn. Lucas had been against selling from the start, and he would never understand why she was considering it. He was so deeply connected to the ranch, to its past, its present, and its future. She didn't want to disappoint him, but she couldn't ignore the harsh realities of running the estate. It was a business, not just a sentimental dream.

Amelia placed the letter down on the desk and ran a hand through her hair, feeling the pressure mounting. She had come to the ranch to escape the city, to find some peace and clarity. Instead, she was trapped between her desire for a fresh start and the weight of the legacy her father had left behind.

The door creaked open, and Lucas stepped inside. His usual confident stride was absent; there was a quiet tension in his posture as his eyes met hers.

"You've been quiet today," he said, his voice low and thoughtful. "Something on your mind?"

Amelia bit her lip, hesitating for a moment before lifting her gaze to meet his. There was a familiarity between them now, a connection that neither of them could ignore. She had come to respect him more than she ever thought she would. But now, that respect was tangled with something deeper, something more dangerous: her growing feelings for him.

"I've been looking over the developer's offer," she said softly, trying to gauge his reaction. "It's... it's tempting, Lucas."

He raised an eyebrow, his gaze sharp. "Tempting? You're seriously considering selling?"

She flinched at the sharpness in his tone. "It's not that simple. The ranch has more debt than we can handle, and we're barely keeping things afloat. I don't know if we can afford to keep going. And then... there's everything else." She motioned to the papers on the desk, the weight of her father's legacy making the air feel heavier.

Lucas walked closer, his expression unreadable. "You're really considering this, aren't you?"

Amelia nodded, her stomach churning with doubt. "I don't want to let go of it, but at the same time, I have to think about the future. My future. I can't let my emotions decide everything. I'm not my father. I can't just keep holding onto this for the sake of some legacy."

Lucas's jaw tightened, and for a moment, the room felt thick with tension. He leaned against the desk, his eyes darkened with frustration.

"I get it," he said after a long silence. "I understand that you have to do what's best for you. But you've been here long enough now to know what this place means. It's not just a piece of property. It's more than that. I know it's been tough, but selling out to that developer—it'll never feel like enough. It'll just be another empty transaction, another thing that's lost."

Amelia felt a flicker of anger. "I know what you're trying to say, Lucas. But it's easy for you to say that. You've spent your whole life here, connected to the land, but I'm not the same as you. I'm not tied to this place. I have my life, my career in the city. This place—this ranch—has been a burden for me, not a gift."

Lucas's face softened, but the hurt in his eyes was undeniable. "I know this isn't easy for you. But this place—it's part of you. You've always been running from it, running from your past, from the weight of what's been left behind. But now, you're here. You're finally facing it."

She took a deep breath, trying to quell the rising tide of emotion. "I'm not sure I can do this anymore, Lucas. I don't know how to balance everything—the ranch, my family's legacy, the pressure from the city—and still figure out who I am. Maybe it's time to let go."

Lucas reached out, his hand gently touching hers. The warmth of his touch sent a shock through her, but she couldn't let herself give in to it. Not now. Not when everything was hanging in the balance.

"Amelia," he said softly, his voice tinged with emotion, "I get that you're scared. But you're not alone in this. I've got your back. We can make it work—together. You don't have to choose between the city and the ranch. You can have both if you let yourself believe in it."

Her heart beat faster at his words, but doubt lingered. "I don't know if I can believe in it, Lucas. I don't know if I can make it work. What if I can't? What if this was never meant to be mine?"

For a moment, Lucas was silent, his grip on her hand tightening. Then, he spoke softly, "If you sell it, you'll never know. But if you stay, you'll have the chance to build something that's yours. Something real. You don't have to do it alone."

Amelia looked into his eyes, searching for the truth in them. She felt the weight of her decision pressing down on her, the anxiety of the unknown gripping her tightly. She had always relied on herself, but now, for the first time in a long while, she realized that maybe—just maybe—she didn't have to carry this burden alone.

The silence between them stretched on as the final decision loomed before her. The developer's offer still stood, but now, with Lucas standing beside her, the choice felt even more complicated.

What if she had been looking for a way out when what she really needed was to trust in the people around her—and herself?

“Give me a little more time,” she whispered, her voice filled with uncertainty. “I need to think.”

Lucas nodded, his expression unreadable, but there was a softness in his eyes that spoke volumes. “Take all the time you need. I’ll be here.”

Amelia turned away, her eyes falling on the papers scattered across the desk. The future of the ranch, her future, was in her hands. And for the first time, she wasn’t sure which way to go. But with Lucas by her side, maybe there was still a chance to make it work.

22

The Unspoken Future

The wind howled outside, the trees bending in the strong gusts, but inside the estate, all was quiet except for the steady rhythm of Amelia's breathing. She sat by the window, her hands folded tightly in her lap, staring out at the sprawling grounds that had been the backdrop of her life in recent days. The rain fell in sheets, the rhythmic drumming of the droplets against the window matching the pounding of her heart.

She was alone. Lucas had gone into town to handle some business matters with the local ranchers, and for once, she was left to her thoughts. A rare occurrence, but one that she knew she needed. There was so much weighing on her mind—so many decisions left to be made. The weight of her future pressed on her chest as she thought of the ranch, her father's legacy, and, most dangerously, Lucas.

For the longest time, she'd kept her feelings buried. The city had always been her world, a world of logic, order, and ambition. Love, at least the kind that took root in the soil of a small town, had always seemed like a distraction. She had been so focused on building her career, on climbing higher, that she never took the time to look at the people around her, to form deeper connections. She didn't have time for it.

But now, staring out at the rain-soaked landscape, it was impossible to ignore the undeniable truth that had crept into her heart. She was in love with Lucas.

The realization was both exhilarating and terrifying. She had tried to deny it for as long as she could, tried to push away the way her heart skipped a beat whenever he smiled or the way she felt the pull of his presence even when he wasn't nearby. But it wasn't just the physical attraction that had kept her tethered to him. No, it was something deeper. He had a way of understanding the land, of seeing the beauty in everything simple, raw, and unpolished. And the way he looked at her—the way his eyes softened when she least expected it—had done something to her. Something she had tried, and failed, to resist.

But there was a problem.

As much as she loved him, she couldn't see how their lives could ever mesh together. She had spent years carving out a life in the city—one filled with board meetings, high-stakes decisions, and a fast-paced lifestyle that was worlds apart from the slower, more grounded existence Lucas embraced on the ranch. She couldn't imagine giving up the city, her career, and everything she had worked for to live the way Lucas did.

Their goals were too different. She wanted to make her mark

in the world, to push boundaries and expand her horizons. He wanted to preserve what had been passed down to him, to keep the ranch alive and thriving, even if it meant resisting the pull of modernization and progress. She wanted to take risks. He preferred the security of tradition. They were like two different worlds, colliding in ways that neither of them could control.

It wasn't just their goals that were at odds—it was their entire existence. She lived in a city where the lights never went out, where every corner had something new to offer, and where ambition could take you anywhere. He lived on a ranch where the days were long, the work was grueling, and the land was what mattered more than anything. Their worlds were as separate as night and day, and yet, here they were, entangled in a way neither could escape.

Sighing, Amelia pushed herself away from the window and moved toward the desk. She had papers scattered across the surface, financial statements for the ranch, lists of expenses, and potential buyers who had shown interest in the land. She could sell. The thought was always there, lurking in the back of her mind, just waiting for the right moment. She could sell the estate and take the money. But the price of that would be far too high.

Could she walk away from Lucas? From the bond they had forged over the past few weeks? From the way he had looked at her, with such tenderness and care, when she was falling apart under the pressure of running the ranch?

Her fingers traced the edge of the papers in front of her, but her thoughts weren't on the numbers. They were on him—on Lucas. He was so much more than the man who had taken over her life in the last few months. He had become someone she could trust, someone who had helped her, taught her, and stood by her when everything seemed like it was falling apart.

But could she be the woman he needed her to be? Could she truly give up everything she had fought for, everything she had built, to become part of his world?

The thought of leaving the city behind was suffocating. It meant giving up her career, her independence, and her dreams. She had always been so sure of what she wanted. But now, with Lucas in the picture, with the ranch calling to her in ways she never expected, everything felt uncertain.

Her thoughts were interrupted by the sound of the door creaking open. She turned quickly, and there he was—Lucas. His figure filled the doorway, his broad shoulders hunched slightly from the wind and rain outside. He looked weary, his clothes damp from the storm, but the moment he stepped into the room, he seemed to bring the outside world with him—a world of fresh air, of possibility, of new beginnings.

Amelia's heart skipped a beat, her feelings for him growing more complicated with each passing day. She had spent so long running from the idea of love, from the idea of tying herself down. But now, as she looked at him, she couldn't deny the truth that had been building inside her for weeks. She was in love with him.

But the words felt impossible to speak. She couldn't just tell him that, not when everything was so uncertain. The ranch, her career, her future—there was too much at stake.

"Amelia," Lucas said softly, his voice carrying a weight that made her stomach twist. "I've been thinking. About everything. About what you've been dealing with. And I need to ask you something."

Her pulse quickened, and she swallowed hard. "What is it?"

He stepped forward, closing the distance between them, his eyes never leaving hers. The air between them felt thick, charged with the tension of everything they had shared.

"I know you've been struggling," he said, his voice softer now. "But I don't want you to think you're in this alone. Whatever decision you make, whatever you choose for the ranch, I'm here. I'll support you."

The sincerity in his voice caught her off guard. For a moment, she forgot about everything else—the ranch, the city, the future. All that mattered was the man standing in front of her, the one who had helped her more than anyone else.

"Lucas," she whispered, her voice cracking. "I don't know what to do. I feel like I'm being torn in two directions, and no matter what I choose, I'll lose something."

"You won't lose me," he said, reaching out to take her hand. "You never will."

His words sent a rush of warmth through her, and for a moment, it felt like everything was right. She didn't have to choose between the city and the ranch. She didn't have to choose between the life she had known and the man she had come to love. The decision was hers to make, but she knew now that no matter what she chose, she wouldn't be alone.

And maybe that was enough.

As Lucas stepped closer, Amelia's heart fluttered in her chest. She was scared—terrified, even—but the pull between them was undeniable. She was in love with him, and there was no denying it any longer.

But the future was still uncertain, and as they stood there, together, Amelia realized that it was no longer just about the ranch or the city. It was about the life she wanted to build, the life she could build—with him.

23

A Fork in the Road

The wind howled outside, slashing against the window panes of the grand estate. The storm had been building all day, the sky darkening as if the heavens themselves were reflecting the turmoil within Amelia. She stood by the window, staring out at the vast expanse of land her father had once ruled with an iron fist, now hers to command—or perhaps, to lose.

The world she had known, the one in the city where everything was at her fingertips, felt like a distant memory, fading away as the days on the ranch stretched into weeks. It was as if she were stuck in a liminal space, neither fully in the past nor ready to step into the future.

Amelia's fingers gripped the edge of the windowsill, her knuckles white. Behind her, the fire crackled, sending tiny bursts of warmth throughout the room. But the heat from the flames was nothing compared to the fire burning inside her—a fire that was slowly consuming her. She had come to this place looking for respite, hoping to escape the chaos of her life, but instead, she had found something more profound and far more dangerous.

Lucas.

Her heart twisted at the thought of him. He had become more than just a man to her—he was a part of her now, and that terrified her. Everything she had worked for, all the years spent carving out a career in the city, had led her to this point. But now, it felt like she was standing at a crossroads, with two paths ahead, and each one leading her away from something she could never go back to.

She thought of the city—her life there was comfortable, predictable, and yet, it always felt empty. She had built her success from the ground up, and yet, every victory seemed to come at the cost of her happiness. The world she had grown accustomed to was full of superficiality, fast-paced decisions, and endless ambition. She had tried to find meaning in it all, but it always felt hollow.

And now, she was here, in a place that demanded something different—something that felt raw and real. The ranch had offered her a refuge, a place where life moved at its own pace. The land, the animals, the workers—it was all so foreign to her, yet it felt more like home than any sleek office or glass skyscraper ever had.

But then, there was Lucas.

Her mind flashed to the night before, when they had stood in the barn, the air thick with tension and unspoken words. He had kissed her—one moment of raw emotion, a moment that left her breathless, conflicted, and uncertain. The kiss had been a promise, a declaration of everything they had built together in the short time she had been there. It had been tender and desperate, as if they were both clinging to something they were too afraid to admit they needed.

She could feel his presence in every corner of the ranch. Lucas wasn't just a man on the property; he was the soul of it, the heart that beat in time with the land. He had grown up here, fought for this land, and now, he was asking her to be a part of it. The thought alone filled her with both longing and dread. She didn't know how to balance the two—her career, her life in the city, and the life Lucas offered her on the ranch.

Could she leave everything behind for him? For the ranch?

The weight of the decision was suffocating. The years she had spent in the city, fighting tooth and nail for every inch of success, made it hard to fathom a life without the bright lights, the endless opportunities, and the stability of her established life. But what had that life truly given her? A career, yes. Success, certainly. But a deep sense of fulfillment? No.

She closed her eyes, letting the silence of the room wash over her. The gentle flicker of the firelight provided the only comfort as she let her thoughts drift back to the way Lucas had held her the night they kissed. It had been a fleeting moment of peace, a release from the internal chaos that had consumed her. But that moment felt so far away now, almost as if it had never happened.

Her heart pounded, and she turned from the window, pacing back and forth across the room. There was no easy answer. Lucas's life was here—on the ranch, with the horses, with the land. He was a part of it, as much as the soil that nourished it. Could she fit into that world? Would she ever truly belong here?

And then there was the matter of the developer's offer. She couldn't ignore it any longer. The future of the ranch was at stake, and the debts her father had left behind loomed large over everything. The offer was tempting—so tempting. It would provide the financial freedom she had always sought, but at what cost? Would she really be able to live with herself, knowing she had let go of everything her father had worked for?

As if on cue, there was a knock at the door. Amelia jumped, her heart racing as she quickly wiped away the tears that had started to form in her eyes. She had been so consumed with her thoughts that she hadn't heard anyone approaching.

"Come in," she called out, her voice steady despite the turmoil inside.

Lucas entered, his presence filling the doorway, his posture relaxed but his eyes serious. He stepped inside, closing the door gently behind him.

"You've been quiet today," he remarked, his voice soft but filled with concern. "Thinking about the offer?"

Amelia nodded, her hands still trembling slightly. She didn't know how to explain the whirlwind of emotions inside her, the chaos she had been feeling since her father's death and the weight of this place settling upon her.

"I don't know what to do, Lucas," she said, her voice trembling. "The offer is... tempting. But it feels wrong. My father left this place to me for a reason, and now I'm supposed to sell it? I don't even know who I am anymore."

Lucas closed the gap between them, his presence grounding her as he gently placed a hand on her arm. "Amelia," he said quietly, "you're not alone in this. I've been here, watching over the land for years. If you choose to stay, I'll help you. But if you choose to go, I'll respect that, too."

Her breath caught in her throat. His words were simple, but they held an undeniable weight. He wasn't just offering her support; he was offering her a choice. A choice that would change everything.

She looked up at him, her heart pounding. "And if I stay? What happens to us?"

Lucas gave her a small, almost imperceptible smile. "We find out together. One step at a time."

Amelia stood there, looking into his eyes, feeling the pressure of the decision closing in on her. There was no turning back now. The ranch, Lucas, the city—her life was at a crossroads, and every road seemed to lead her in a different direction.

But as she stood there with Lucas, the quiet weight of the moment wrapping around them both, Amelia realized something. It wasn't the ranch that held her captive—it was the choice. The decision that would shape her future, her heart, and the life she wanted to build.

"I'll figure it out," she said, her voice filled with resolve. "But right now, I need time."

Lucas nodded, his hand still resting gently on her arm. "Take all the time you need, Amelia. I'll be here, whatever you decide."

The weight of her decision was far from over, but as she looked into his eyes, for the first time in what felt like forever, Amelia didn't feel alone. Maybe, just maybe, she could find a way to make it all work.

24

A Moment of Clarity

The sun dipped low in the sky, casting long shadows across the rolling fields of the ranch. Amelia stood on the porch of the main house, the cool breeze tugging at her hair. She hadn't noticed how beautiful the land was until now. Each day that passed, she felt more connected to it, as though the land itself was calling to her, grounding her in a way that the flashing lights of the city never could.

She had always thought her happiness was tied to her career, to the fast-paced world of law and high-rise buildings. But now, as she watched the horses graze in the distance, as she listened to the soft rustling of the trees, Amelia realized that everything she had ever wanted might not be what she thought it was.

The ranch had always felt like a burden. Her father had left her with an inheritance she hadn't asked for, a life that seemed so far removed from her own. But as the weeks went on, as she struggled with the ranch's future and her place in it, something had shifted inside of her. It wasn't just the work that needed to be done. It was the people—Lucas, the ranch workers, even the land itself. She had been running for so long, running from the responsibilities her father had left her, running from the pain of her past, and running from the idea that her happiness could ever be anything other than an illusion.

But now, standing here, Amelia felt something different—a sense of calm. The noise of the world felt distant, almost muffled. The tension that had gripped her since her arrival had loosened, replaced by a quiet understanding that she was exactly where she needed to be.

Amelia turned as the door opened behind her, and Lucas stepped out onto the porch. His rugged figure was outlined by the fading sunlight, the lines of his face softening in the golden glow. His presence was a constant—like the land itself—and with each passing day, she found herself relying on him more and more, not just for help with the ranch, but for the emotional support he offered without even trying.

"You're quiet today," Lucas said, his voice low, with an undercurrent of concern. "You've been out here a while."

"I was just thinking," she said, offering him a small, uncertain smile. She didn't know why, but today felt different—like a turning point.

"About what?" Lucas asked, stepping closer to her. His eyes searched hers as if trying to read her thoughts. There was something in the way he looked at her that always made her feel exposed but in the best way possible. It was as though he was the only one who truly saw her—her fears, her uncertainties, and the pieces of her that she had spent so long hiding.

"I don't know," she said, shaking her head. "It's just that everything feels... clearer today. I've been so focused on the future—on what's next—that I didn't stop to appreciate where I am right now. I think I've been running from it, not just from the ranch, but from what it represents. From my past, from my father's expectations, and... from you."

Lucas raised an eyebrow, his expression unreadable. "From me?"

Amelia nodded, the weight of her words hanging in the air between them. "I didn't realize how much I had been running until now. I thought I was running from the responsibility of the ranch, but really, I was running from the idea that my happiness might not be found in the city, in the career I've built, or in the life I've been living for all these years. Maybe my happiness is right here, in front of me."

Lucas remained silent, his eyes locked on hers, his face softening as he took a step closer. "Amelia," he said softly, his voice laced with something she couldn't quite identify, "you don't have to decide anything right now. I know the decision you're facing is big. But you've already made a choice, even if you haven't realized it yet."

Amelia felt a lump rise in her throat at his words. "What do you mean?" she asked, her voice barely above a whisper.

"You've already chosen to stay," Lucas said, his voice gentle but firm. "You've already chosen this place. You're not just here because of your father's will, or because of some obligation. You're here because a part of you wants to be. You've made this ranch your own, in your way, and I can see it. I've seen it in the way you've fought for it, in the way you've cared for the animals, and in the way you've opened up to me. Your heart is here now, Amelia. You just need to see it."

The words hit her like a wave, washing over her with such force that for a moment, she couldn't breathe. It was true. Everything he said was true. She had come here thinking she was doing it out of obligation, thinking that the ranch was just a thing she had to fix before moving on with her life. But in that moment, standing in the golden light with Lucas, she understood that she had already chosen this place. She had chosen the ranch, and she had chosen him.

Her heart hammered in her chest as she stepped closer to him, her fingers trembling slightly as she reached out. "I don't know what this means for us, Lucas," she said, her voice barely audible. "I don't know how I can make this work. But... I can't deny what I feel."

Lucas didn't hesitate. He closed the distance between them, his hands gently cupping her face as he kissed her forehead, tender and reassuring. "You don't have to know everything right now. We'll figure it out together. One step at a time."

At that moment, Amelia realized that she didn't need all the answers. She didn't need to figure out her entire future, because the future wasn't something she could control. The only thing she needed was to trust herself—and Lucas—and take the next step, whatever it might be.

"I'm ready," she whispered, her voice filled with certainty. "I'm ready to stay. I'm ready to make this my home."

Lucas smiled, his expression softening as he kissed her lips, a kiss that was full of promise. It was a kiss that said they were in this together—whatever the future held, they would face it side by side.

And as the sky darkened, as the first stars began to twinkle above, Amelia knew that this was the beginning of something new. Something real. Something that could finally fill the emptiness she had been running from for so long.

She had found her place, and it was right here—with him.

25

The Decision

Amelia stood at the edge of the ranch, looking out at the vast land her family had worked so hard to cultivate. The evening sky was tinged with shades of purple and gold as the sun dipped below the horizon, casting long shadows over the fields. The wind, crisp and cool, swept through the tall grass, and she inhaled deeply as if trying to inhale all the possibilities that lay before her. This land, the land her father had built his life around, was now hers to protect, and it had become more than just an inheritance. It was a part of her, just as much as she had become a part of it.

The developer's offer still sat heavily on her mind. She had thought about it endlessly over the past week, unable to shake the tempting promise of a future free from the weight of responsibility. The money they were offering for the ranch was more than enough to secure her future, to secure a life of ease, of luxury. She could walk away, return to the city, and forget about this place—forget about the struggles, the memories, the legacy her father had left behind.

But every time she considered that path, she felt a pang of guilt, as if the very act of considering it was a betrayal. A betrayal to her father's memory, to the people who had worked this land for generations, and to herself. Her heart beat louder in her chest, drowning out the whispers of temptation. The city, with all its allure, was not where she belonged. She had come here to escape the noise, to find something real, and now she realized that her happiness would never be found by running away.

Her thoughts were interrupted by a soft sound behind her, and she turned to see Lucas walking toward her. He looked as solid and grounded as ever, his presence like a pillar of support that anchored her in a way she never thought possible. The briefest of smiles crossed his face as he reached her, his eyes searching hers with a mixture of concern and understanding.

"You've been out here for a while," he said, his voice calm but full of unspoken questions. "Thinking about the offer?"

Amelia nodded, her gaze returning to the horizon. She didn't need to answer. Lucas knew exactly what she was struggling with. He had been patient, understanding, and unwavering in his belief that she had the strength to make the right decision. But this was her decision to make, and for the first time, she wasn't afraid of the weight it carried.

"I don't know what to do, Lucas," she confessed, her voice barely above a whisper. "The offer is everything I could have wanted. Financial security, a way out of all of this. But... I don't think I can just sell it. I don't think I can turn my back on something my father built."

Lucas stepped closer to her, his hands settling on her shoulders in a comforting gesture. His touch was steady, grounding her amid the turmoil she felt.

"Amelia," he said, his voice gentle but firm. "You don't have to choose what's easy. What matters is what you truly want. This land means something to you. It's in your blood, and it's in your heart. I can see it. You've already made your decision. You just need to believe in it."

The words settled over her like a warm blanket, and Amelia let out a slow breath. For the first time in days, she allowed herself to admit it. The ranch wasn't just something to inherit or sell off. It was her legacy too, and it was worth fighting for. She wasn't just going to walk away from it. She was going to make it thrive again, to rebuild what had been lost, and to honor everything her father had worked for.

"I'm going to turn it down," Amelia said, her voice steady now. "I'm going to fight for this place, for the people who depend on it. I can't sell out. I can't just walk away."

Lucas' eyes softened, a flicker of pride passing through them. "I knew you'd make the right choice."

A small smile tugged at the corners of her lips as she turned to face him fully. "I couldn't have done it without you," she said, her voice quieter now, but full of sincerity. "You've helped me see things I couldn't see before. You've given me a reason to believe in this place again, in myself."

Lucas stepped forward, his hands sliding from her shoulders to her arms, pulling her close. His expression softened, and his lips brushed hers in a slow, lingering kiss. Amelia melted into the kiss, feeling the weight of everything she had been holding inside release in that one moment. The kiss wasn't just an expression of attraction, it was a promise—one that they would face whatever came next, together.

When they broke apart, Amelia's heart raced in her chest. There was so much ahead of them, so many obstacles still to face. But for the first time, she felt like she wasn't alone. For the first time, she knew that no matter what, she had Lucas by her side.

"Thank you," she whispered, her fingers tracing his jawline, feeling the rough stubble beneath her fingertips.

Lucas smiled, his eyes never leaving hers. "There's nothing to thank me for. You're the one who made the decision. You're the one who's going to rebuild this ranch, make it your own."

Amelia's heart swelled with gratitude and something deeper—a sense of belonging, of purpose. She had made the right choice. The ranch was hers to protect, and she was going to fight for it.

As the sun dipped below the horizon, casting long shadows across the land, Amelia felt a weight lift from her shoulders. She wasn't just facing the future anymore. She was embracing it, with Lucas by her side. Together, they would make this place thrive again.

For the first time since her arrival, Amelia felt at peace. The decision had been made. She wasn't running anymore. She was home.

26

The Cost of Change

The morning air was crisp and cool as Amelia stood in the middle of the estate, watching the workers move in every direction with purpose. The ranch was alive with activity—every corner of the land was being tended to, worked on, or cleared in preparation for the upcoming season. For the first time, Amelia felt like she was part of something larger than herself. She had decided to fight for this place, for the legacy of her family, and the realization that the ranch was her responsibility had become more real with each passing day.

But despite the newfound sense of purpose, the challenges had not gotten easier. It was the cost of change—of transformation—and Amelia was learning quickly that true change, especially when it came to a place like this, did not come without sacrifice.

"You're pushing them too hard," Lucas's voice broke through her thoughts, sharp but not unkind.

Amelia turned to see him walking toward her, his hand wiping the sweat from his brow. His shirt was tucked in, but she could see the strain in his posture, a reflection of the intensity of the work they had been doing. There were days when it felt as though the weight of everything was on their shoulders, and today was no exception. There had been so many changes to implement, so many things to fix, and it felt like the ranch was an endless, never-ending task.

"I'm not pushing them too hard," Amelia said, her voice defensive but not angry. "This place needs to be fixed, Lucas. We have no choice. If we don't get it back in shape, we'll lose everything."

"I know," Lucas said, his voice softening. "But you're burning yourself out, and you're burning the crew out too. You've got to give them time. Rome wasn't built in a day, and this ranch isn't going to be saved overnight."

Amelia knew he was right, but the pressure was overwhelming. She had come back to the ranch to escape the stress of the city, but the responsibility of running this place was weighing on her like a boulder. Every decision, every misstep, felt like it could push her closer to failure. But in her heart, she knew that this place could be something again. It could thrive if she could just hold it together long enough to make the right moves. But that was the problem—she wasn't sure how long she had before the ranch was gone.

"I can't afford to slow down now," she said, her voice tight. "I can't let it fall apart."

Lucas stepped closer to her, his expression earnest. "You don't have to do this alone, Amelia. We're in this together, remember?"

"I know," she replied, taking a deep breath. "But I don't know how much more I can give. Every day it feels like one more thing goes wrong, and I'm running out of ideas."

Lucas placed a hand on her shoulder, his grip strong and comforting. "I know it's hard. But you're not alone. And we'll make it through this. The ranch, the workers, the future—it's all going to work out. Just take it one step at a time."

His words were reassuring, but the truth was, that Amelia felt like she was walking a tightrope with no safety net beneath her. She had come here to save the ranch, but she didn't know if she was strong enough to carry the weight of it all.

Over the next few weeks, Amelia and Lucas continued to pour everything they had into the ranch. They met with the local farmers and ranchers to create partnerships, put together plans to restructure the operations, and began reaching out to investors who might be willing to help fund the restoration. But no matter how many steps they took forward, there was always the looming threat of failure. Every conversation with a potential investor felt like a negotiation for her very soul—would they save the ranch, or would she be forced to sell?

Meanwhile, Amelia continued to learn the nuances of running a ranch. She spent her mornings in meetings, her afternoons walking the grounds, and her evenings poring over spreadsheets and business reports. She was beginning to understand more about the land and the animals than she ever thought she would. But the sacrifices were mounting. She had to make decisions she never imagined herself making—decisions that impacted her future and the lives of the workers on the ranch. And each time she made one, she wondered if it would be the one that pushed everything over the edge.

One evening, after a long day of meetings and planning, Amelia sat at her desk, the office quiet except for the soft clinking of the grandfather clock in the corner. She ran a hand through her hair, fatigue settling deep in her bones. Her phone buzzed on the desk, and she reached for it absently, not expecting anything urgent.

It was a message from her business associate in the city—one she had left behind when she'd decided to come to the ranch. The message was short but clear:

"The real estate developer is making one last push for the land. He'll make an offer that's impossible to refuse. Don't wait too long."

Amelia's heart skipped a beat as she read the message. She had known this moment would come. She had known that the developer would eventually push harder, offering more money than she could ever imagine. The numbers they had put on the table had been staggering, enough to secure her future, enough to give her the life she had always wanted. But it would mean giving up the ranch—the very thing she had come to love and fight for.

She sat back in her chair, staring at the screen, the weight of the decision sinking in. The temptation to walk away, to accept the offer and get out while she still had the chance, was overwhelming. She could go back to the city, back to the world she knew so well. She could leave the struggles behind, leave the debt, leave the burden of responsibility.

But something inside her hesitated. Something deep inside her knew that she had to make a choice that aligned with who she had become. This ranch, the land, the workers—they were all part of her now. It was no longer about the city, the career, the easy life. It was about this place, and what it had come to mean to her.

She wasn't ready to give up.

Lucas entered the office quietly, his presence filling the room. He could see the tension on her face as she stared at the message on her phone, and he knew exactly what it was. He walked over to her, placing a hand on her shoulder. She didn't look up, but she didn't need to. He already knew.

"You're thinking about it, aren't you?" he asked softly.

Amelia nodded slowly. "The offer's still there. They want to buy. And they're offering a lot more than I ever thought I'd see. I don't know if I can turn that down. But then... I look at the ranch, and I can't imagine letting it go. I've worked so hard to make this work. And I'm scared that if I give in, I'll lose everything."

Lucas's grip tightened on her shoulder. "I know it's hard. But you have to ask yourself—what do you want for yourself? Not for the business, not for anyone else—what's right for you?"

Amelia sat silently for a long moment, the weight of the decision pressing down on her. She knew Lucas was right. This wasn't about anyone else. It wasn't about the money or the offers. It was about what she could live with. She could either walk away from everything and secure her future, or she could fight for the ranch—and everything it meant to her.

Slowly, Amelia set the phone down and stood up. She turned to face Lucas, her expression firm. "I'm not giving up. I'm going to fight. For the ranch, for my family's legacy, for everything this place stands for. I'm not walking away."

Lucas smiled, pride flickering in his eyes. "That's the Amelia I've always known."

And in that moment, Amelia knew. She wasn't just fighting for the ranch anymore. She was fighting for her own future—one that she would shape, one that she could be proud of. The decision had been made.

They would rebuild it together.

27

The Family Reunion

The air in the drawing room of the Pierce family estate was thick with tension, and Amelia could feel the weight of it pressing on her chest. The house, still grand despite the years of neglect, felt empty—silent, as though holding its breath in anticipation. She stood by the window, watching the clouds roll across the sky, her fingers drumming nervously against the old, worn wood of the sill.

The phone call had been brief, a simple invitation extended to her estranged family. But now, standing in the room where she had spent much of her childhood, everything seemed to have changed. This wasn't the home she remembered, not really. The years of distance, the choices she had made, and the pain she had buried all led her here today. The ranch—her last connection to her father's legacy—was where she had decided to rebuild, but first, she needed the support of the people who had always been there, even if they hadn't been present.

She heard the knock before she could think. The door creaked open slowly, and her heart jumped in her chest. In walked her mother, Sarah Pierce, followed closely by her older brother, William. Amelia hadn't seen either of them in years—not since her departure to the city, not since she had turned her back on this life. The years had not been kind to her mother's once-vibrant face, now etched with lines of worry, but the same fire burned in her eyes. William, on the other hand, looked as confident and distant as ever—his posture stiff, his arms folded in a silent defense.

"Amelia," her mother spoke first, her voice tight.

Amelia turned from the window to face them. "Mother. William." The words felt foreign, almost mechanical. "Thank you for coming."

There was an awkward pause. Amelia expected no less. The distance between them was evident, but she couldn't help but feel a flicker of hope. Maybe this was a step forward. Maybe, after all this time, they could find common ground.

Her mother stepped into the room, her eyes never leaving Amelia. "I didn't think you'd ask us to come back here. Especially after everything that happened."

Amelia winced, but she steadied herself. "I didn't expect it to be easy," she said. "But we have unfinished business, Mom. The estate, the ranch... and the future." She hesitated, taking a breath. "I need your help."

William remained silent, arms crossed, his gaze cold as he

surveyed the room. It wasn't lost on Amelia that he had never truly understood her decisions, nor had he ever agreed with her departure from their family's way of life. The gap between them felt as wide as it ever had.

"I'm surprised you want anything to do with this place," William finally spoke, his tone dripping with skepticism. "After all these years of building your career in the city, now you want us to help with the ranch?"

"I never wanted to leave," Amelia shot back, her voice rising just a little. "You know that, William. But sometimes, life doesn't let you stay where you want."

Her mother nodded slowly, though her lips remained tightly pressed. "It's not that simple, Amelia. You've been gone for a long time. And this place... the ranch... it's different now. It's been neglected. You've probably seen that for yourself."

Amelia winced, her heart sinking. Her mother's words were true, but the bitter sting of it all still hurt. "I know. I'm doing everything I can to turn things around."

Her mother looked at her with a mixture of sadness and resignation. "You've always been stubborn. I never doubted that you'd try to fix things. But the ranch is more than just land and property. It's about the family, about legacy. Your father would have wanted you to preserve it, but it's not an easy job."

The mention of her father's name stirred something deep within Amelia, something raw and untamed. She had spent so many years blaming him for everything—blaming him for the ranch, for the inheritance, for the obligation that had once felt so suffocating. But now, standing here, in front of the family she had tried to forget, she realized how much she missed him. The pain of his loss still lingered, and she could feel it like a weight on her chest.

"I know it's not easy," she said softly, her voice faltering slightly. "But I want to give it a chance. The ranch... our family's legacy means something to me. It always has."

William stepped forward, breaking the silence that had enveloped the room. "Amelia, you don't understand. This place, this family... it's not what you think it is. You left us behind, and now you're coming back, asking for our help. We don't even know where you stand anymore." His voice was tight with frustration, but it was also tinged with hurt.

Amelia met his gaze, the fire in her eyes matching his. "I didn't leave you, William. I left because I didn't have a choice. I thought I was doing what was best for all of us. I thought I was leaving the past behind to create something better for myself." She paused, swallowing the lump in her throat. "But I realize now, I was wrong."

A tense silence settled between them. Amelia could feel the weight of her confession—how it changed everything, how it made the years of separation feel almost irrelevant. The years of misunderstanding, of anger, of pride—they had built walls that had kept them apart, but now, standing in front of each other, Amelia was starting to wonder if those walls could finally come down.

Her mother's expression softened. "I know you think you can fix this, Amelia. But this place—it's not just your burden to bear. It's our burden too."

Amelia nodded slowly, her heart heavy. "I know. I need your help. I can't do this alone."

She had been fighting this battle for so long—fighting against the responsibility, the pressure, the weight of her father's legacy. But now, in the quiet of this room, she knew it was time to stop fighting. It was time to rebuild. Not just the ranch, but the family she had tried to forget, the family she still longed for.

"Fine," William said, his voice softening. "But it's not going to be easy. You can't just waltz in and expect things to go back to normal. We have a lot to work through. We need to make some decisions about the future."

Amelia met his eyes, feeling the burden of his words but also a flicker of hope. "I know. And I'm ready to do whatever it takes."

The reunion, however tense, had sparked something inside Amelia—a recognition that she didn't have to carry this burden alone. Her family, though fractured, was still hers. The walls were cracking. Slowly but surely, they were beginning to rebuild what had been lost.

"Alright," her mother said with a sigh, a slight smile tugging at her lips. "Let's start by figuring out what comes next."

As Amelia looked at the family she had left behind, she knew that this was just the beginning. There would be challenges ahead, both with the ranch and with the family she had once distanced herself from. But as she stood there, surrounded by the echoes of her past and the possibility of a new future, she finally understood—she wasn't in this alone anymore.

And maybe, just maybe, the ranch and the family were worth fighting for.

28

The Final Test

The morning air was crisp as Amelia stood by the window of the study, gazing out over the vast expanse of the ranch. The sun had barely risen, casting a golden glow over the rolling hills and open pastures. It should have been a beautiful sight—a quiet morning to reflect on the progress she had made. But today was different. Today, everything was on the line.

Behind her, the faint sound of footsteps alerted Amelia to Lucas's presence. He stood in the doorway, his face drawn with concern, his usually confident demeanor replaced by something darker.

"Have you seen the papers?" he asked, his voice low.

Amelia didn't answer right away. She didn't need to. The moment she'd picked up the phone that morning, the reality of the situation had hit her. The developer, Thomas Harrington, wasn't going to play fair anymore. He wasn't content with the polite offers and legal negotiations—they had tried that route for months. Now, he had moved to more aggressive tactics, launching a smear campaign designed to break her resolve.

"I saw," she said softly, turning to face him. "He's not giving up, is he?"

Lucas stepped into the room, his eyes flickering with frustration. "No, he's not. He's playing dirty now. Trying to turn everyone against you."

Amelia could feel her pulse quicken, her hands clenched at her sides. The familiar feeling of being cornered, of having no way out, surged within her. She had fought so hard to hold onto the ranch, to make her father proud, and now it felt like it was slipping from her grasp.

"We knew this was coming," she murmured, trying to steady her racing thoughts. "But I didn't expect him to resort to this."

Lucas's gaze softened, and for a moment, his expression seemed more vulnerable than she had ever seen it. "I never expected this, either. But we can't let him win. We can't let him take what we've built."

She swallowed the lump in her throat. The future of the ranch had never been more uncertain. They were fighting not just for the land, but for everything they had worked for, for everything that had come to mean something in her life. The memories of her father, the ties to the land, the hard work that had gone into keeping the ranch alive—it all hung in the balance.

“You’ve always believed in this place,” Amelia said, her voice barely a whisper. “In us.”

Lucas didn’t answer immediately. Instead, he stepped forward and took her hand, his grip firm, a silent promise in his touch. “I’m not backing down. Neither should you.”

But Amelia knew it wasn’t just about fighting for the land. It wasn’t just about standing her ground. It was about everything—the past, the future, and, most importantly, the life they were both trying to build.

“I don’t know if I can win this fight,” she said, the words escaping before she could stop them.

Lucas’s face hardened, but there was a flicker of something else in his eyes—something determined, something unwavering. “I’m not asking you to do this alone. We fight together, Amelia. We’ll fight him at every turn.”

Her heart raced in her chest as she looked at him. She had never seen him so resolute, so willing to risk everything. The trust between them, though still fragile at times, had grown over the months. They had fought side by side, survived personal struggles, and now, here they were again—on the cusp of something that could change everything.

Amelia knew this fight was more than just about the ranch. It was about their future together, and she had to decide if she was willing to take that leap—if she was willing to risk everything to save not just the land, but the life they had built. The connection they shared. The love they were starting to acknowledge, no matter how much they tried to resist it.

"I'm with you," she said, her voice stronger now. "Let's do this."

Lucas gave her a small, approving nod. "Good. We'll need to go public. We'll need to show everyone just who Thomas Harrington really is."

The plan was set. They knew the risks. Going public meant more scrutiny, more challenges, and more enemies. But if they didn't act now, they would lose everything.

The rest of the day was spent preparing. They gathered evidence of the developer's underhanded tactics—illegal deals, fraudulent promises, attempts to bribe officials. Amelia's fingers flew over the keyboard, her mind working faster than ever as she pieced everything together. Every email, every contract, every conversation with the local government officials—everything was used to expose Harrington for who he was.

By the time the evening rolled around, they had a solid case. The media would be on their side, they hoped. The press conference they'd planned would reveal the truth about the real estate mogul, showing the public the depths of his manipulation. The ranch, the land, the legacy—it all rested on their ability to stand tall and expose the developer's greed.

As the sun dipped below the horizon, Amelia stood by the window again, looking out over the ranch. The air was thick with tension, and she felt a knot tighten in her stomach. The battle was far from over, but she had one more chance to protect everything that mattered. To protect Lucas.

"We'll do it tomorrow," Lucas said, his voice low behind her. "It's the right time. No more delays."

Amelia turned to face him, her heart pounding. "And if it doesn't work? What if he comes for us anyway?"

"We'll deal with it then," Lucas replied, his eyes meeting hers with a fierce intensity. "Together."

For a long moment, neither of them spoke. The weight of the world seemed to rest on their shoulders, but in that silence, Amelia knew that they were stronger together. Whatever happened next, she wouldn't be alone.

The storm they were about to weather was far from predictable, but Amelia knew one thing for sure: She was ready to face it. She was ready to fight for what was hers—what they had built together.

The final test had arrived, and the battle for the future of the ranch, for their lives, was about to begin.

Tomorrow. The world would know the truth.

29

New Beginnings

The sun had barely risen over the ranch, casting a soft golden light across the fields. Amelia stood at the edge of the porch, her fingers wrapped around a warm cup of coffee, feeling the cool morning breeze on her skin. She had always loved the mornings here, even before she had embraced the ranch as her own. Now, it felt different—more meaningful.

Lucas stepped out from the kitchen, wiping his hands on a dishtowel. His shirt sleeves were rolled up, a sign that the day's work had already begun. But there was a difference in him today. Gone was the intensity that had often made him seem like a man carrying the weight of the world. Today, he stood a little taller, his eyes a little brighter, as if everything had finally fallen into place.

"Morning," he said, walking toward her, a quiet smile playing at the corners of his lips.

"Morning," she replied, smiling back. She watched as he

approached, and for a moment, the world seemed to stand still. The worries, the battles they had fought, everything faded away. It was just the two of them, standing in the early light, beginning a new chapter.

"We've got a lot to do today," Lucas said, glancing at the horizon, his voice taking on a practical tone. "But I thought we'd take a minute. You know, just... breathe."

Amelia's heart swelled at the simple sentiment. He had been her rock through everything—the battles with the developer, the emotional struggles, and even the times when it felt like they were on the edge of losing everything. And now, here they were, with the ranch saved, and their future wide open.

"Breathe," she repeated softly, taking in the fresh air. "I like the sound of that."

For the first time in months, she felt peace settle in her chest. The ranch was hers—not just by inheritance, but by choice. She wasn't the outsider anymore; this place was part of her, just as it was a part of Lucas. They had fought side by side to protect it, and they had won. Now, it was time to rebuild.

"I've been thinking about the future," she said, her voice steady but with a hint of uncertainty. "About what comes next."

Lucas leaned against the railing, his gaze fixed on the horizon. "You're thinking about the ranch, I assume?"

"Part of it," Amelia replied. She took a deep breath and met his eyes. "But also about us. What comes next for us."

Lucas turned his head to look at her, his expression softening. He had been patient with her, letting her process everything at her own pace. But now, as she looked at him, there was no hesitation in her heart. She had fallen for him—truly, deeply—and it was no longer something she could hide.

"We've been through a lot," she continued, "and I know there's still so much to do. But I can't help but wonder... what do we build now? What do we do now that we've survived this storm?"

Lucas smiled then, a small, knowing smile, one that reached his eyes. "We build something worth fighting for," he said quietly. "Together."

His words lingered between them, and for a moment, Amelia felt the full weight of their significance. They had fought for this—this ranch, their love, their future—and now, they were in the position to shape that future. It wasn't about wealth or status anymore. It was about what truly mattered: the love they shared, the dreams they had, and the commitment to make those dreams a reality.

"I've been thinking about that too," she said softly, feeling her heart swell as she spoke. "I know the ranch needs work, and I'm committed to seeing it thrive. But I also think... I think we should take it slow. There's so much we can do here, but there's a bigger world out there too. A world I want to experience with you."

Lucas's eyes brightened, and for a moment, she saw the glimmer of something in him—a hope, a longing. "You're talking about more than just this place, aren't you?"

She nodded, her gaze steady on him. "I am. I want to see what's out there. To travel, to experience the world together. To build something more than just a ranch. I want us to live a life that's more than the struggles and the work. A life that's full of joy, and freedom, and love."

Lucas's lips parted, but before he could respond, Amelia reached out and took his hand, squeezing it gently. "I'm not saying we abandon the ranch. It's part of us now. But I want more than just this. I want a life with you, Lucas. A real life. Together."

He was silent for a moment, his thumb gently tracing the back of her hand. The weight of his thoughts hung in the air, and Amelia could feel his internal struggle. This was more than just a conversation about their future; this was about the life they would build—and it was the first time either of them had truly acknowledged the full scope of it.

Finally, Lucas spoke, his voice low but steady. "You know, I've always believed in this place. I've always believed in the ranch, and in what we could build here. But you're right. There's a whole world out there, a world I want to see with you. A world that's not just about work or survival, but about living."

Amelia's heart raced as she heard his words. It was what she had longed to hear, but she hadn't dared hope he would agree. And yet, here they were, standing on the edge of a new beginning, ready to step forward together.

"I've never really had the chance to think about it before," he continued, his hand tightening around hers. "But now, with you, I see it. I see a future. Not just for the ranch, but for us. We can have both, Amelia. We can have this place, and we can have the world. We just have to make it happen."

She smiled, a tear slipping down her cheek. She hadn't realized how much she needed to hear those words until now. For so long, it had been about survival. About fighting. But now, it was about living. And she had the man she loved standing beside her, ready to build something together.

"I think we've already made it happen," Amelia whispered, her voice full of hope and certainty. "One step at a time."

Lucas leaned in then, his lips brushing against hers in a soft, lingering kiss. The kiss was filled with the weight of everything they had fought for, everything they had endured—and everything they were now ready to create together.

When they pulled apart, Lucas looked at her with a look that could melt the world. "We're just getting started," he said softly.

Amelia smiled, feeling the world shift beneath her feet most perfectly. They had come through the storm, together. And now, they could face whatever came next—together.

As the sun rose higher, casting its golden rays across the ranch, Amelia and Lucas stood side by side, ready to take on the world. The future was uncertain, but it was theirs to shape. And they would shape it together, no matter what.

30

The Heart's Choice

The warm breeze stirred the leaves of the old oak tree outside, creating a soft rustling sound that mingled with the distant calls of birds. The smell of fresh grass and earth filled the air, bringing a sense of calm that Amelia hadn't felt in years. She stood on the porch of the ranch house, her fingers curled around the railing as she looked out over the sprawling fields. The sun was just beginning to dip beneath the horizon, casting an orange glow over everything in sight.

It had been a long road to get here. Amelia had never imagined that she would return to this place, let alone become a part of it again. The city had always been her home, a place of ambition and success, where every move was calculated, and every decision made for the sake of progress. But here, standing on the porch with the cool evening air on her face, she realized that what she had built in the city didn't compare to what she had now.

Her gaze shifted to the stables, where she could just make out the figure of Lucas working with the horses. His movements were steady and confident, his connection with the land and animals undeniable. She had watched him for weeks, learning more about him than she ever thought possible. Lucas wasn't just a rancher; he was a man of quiet strength, someone who lived by principles that didn't revolve around power or money.

Her heart swelled with a mix of emotions. The journey they had taken together had been one of discovery—about herself, about the ranch, and Lucas. She had fought against her feelings, pushed back against the life she had once known and tried to reconcile the woman she was with the woman she had become.

But now, with everything that had happened—the struggles, the setbacks, the victories—she knew she had to make a choice. The city, with all its distractions and temptations, no longer called to her the way it once had. The business world she had conquered seemed small in comparison to the life she had created here, in the quiet expanse of the ranch, surrounded by people who knew the true meaning of hard work and resilience.

And then there was Lucas. He had become her anchor, the one person who had shown her a different way to live, to love, and to be. Their relationship had gone through fire, each challenge revealing new layers of their connection. They had fought together, laughed together, and in many ways, they had healed each other. But the biggest challenge still lay ahead.

Amelia turned away from the porch and walked toward the stables, her heart beating faster with every step. She had made up her mind. No more running. No more holding back. It was time to let go of the past and embrace the future. But the decision wasn't simple. She knew it would change everything—her relationship with Lucas, her life here, and the person she was becoming.

As she entered the stables, she found Lucas brushing down one of the horses, his back to her. The sight of him—calm, focused, and at peace with the world—made her heart ache with the realization of how much she needed him. He had become her safe place, her constant, and the thought of losing that made the decision feel even harder.

"Hey," she said softly, and Lucas turned around, a smile tugging at the corners of his lips when he saw her.

"Hey yourself," he replied, setting the brush down and walking toward her. "Everything okay?"

Amelia hesitated, her breath catching in her throat. The moment felt heavier than she had expected, the weight of her decision pressing on her shoulders. She knew she couldn't keep holding on to the past. It was time to step forward.

"I've been thinking a lot lately," she began, her voice steady but filled with emotion. "About everything... this place, my life, what I want, what we want."

Lucas raised an eyebrow, his expression softening with understanding. He reached out, taking her hand in his. "You don't have to say anything you're not ready to."

But Amelia shook her head. This time, she was ready.

"I'm ready," she said, her voice growing stronger with each word. "I've spent so much of my life thinking that success meant building something in the city, being someone people admired. But I don't think that's who I am anymore, Lucas. The city isn't my home anymore. This place is. With you."

Lucas looked at her with a mixture of surprise and relief. "Amelia..."

"I can't keep living in two worlds," she continued, squeezing his hand. "I can't keep trying to hold on to something that doesn't fit anymore. This"—she gestured to the ranch, to the land, to them—"this is where I belong. And I want to build something here. With you."

Lucas's eyes softened, and he stepped closer to her. The space between them seemed to disappear as he gently cupped her face in his hands. "You don't know how long I've wanted to hear you say that," he whispered, his voice thick with emotion. "I know it's not easy, and I know it wasn't what you expected, but I'm so glad you're here. I've never wanted anything more than to have you by my side, in this life."

Tears welled up in her eyes as she smiled up at him. She had come so far, and now, she was ready to embrace the future—her future, their future. The weight of her decision felt lighter now that she had voiced it aloud.

"I've been scared, Lucas," she admitted, her voice barely above a whisper. “Scared of giving up everything I’ve worked for, scared of losing myself in this life. But I realized... I never really had myself until now. And I want to build a life with you. Not just here, but wherever life takes us.”

Lucas leaned down, his forehead resting against hers. “You’re not going to lose yourself. You’re just going to find a part of you that was always waiting to be found.”

They stood there for a moment, their breaths mingling, their hearts beating in synchrony. It felt like everything had led to this moment, this realization that they were ready to step into the future together, side by side.

“I’m ready,” Amelia said, her voice steady with conviction. “I’m ready to build a life with you. Here. Together.”

Lucas smiled, his eyes shining with something deep and unspoken. “Then we’ll do it. We’ll build it together.”

And with that, everything shifted. The uncertainty that had plagued her for so long melted away, replaced by a sense of clarity she hadn’t known she was missing. She had made her choice. She had chosen him, and in choosing him, she had found herself.

As the sun dipped lower on the horizon, casting a golden glow over the ranch, Amelia knew that this was just the beginning. There would be challenges ahead, but they would face them together. And that was all that mattered.

Hand in hand, they turned toward the future—one full of love, dreams, and possibilities. Together.

31

The Legacy Restored

The morning mist clung to the rolling hills of the ranch like a veil, softening the sharp edges of reality and giving everything an ethereal glow. Amelia stood at the edge of the barn, looking out over the fields that stretched toward the horizon. There was something about the land that always grounded her, the way the earth seemed to hum with life, as if every blade of grass, every tree, had its own story to tell.

She drew in a deep breath, letting the cool, fresh air fill her lungs. Her fingers instinctively tightened around the leather reins of the horse she'd just saddled. It had been a long journey—one that had pushed her to the edge, forced her to confront her fears and doubts, and ultimately led her here, standing on the land that was meant to be her legacy. The ranch was more than just property. It was her family's history, her father's dreams, and now, her future.

Lucas's voice pulled her from her thoughts. "You're going to wear yourself out just standing there, you know."

She turned to see him approaching, his weathered boots kicking up the dust as he walked. He wore a wide grin, the same grin that had become so familiar to her, the one that held so much warmth and promise. He was dressed in his usual ranch attire, his shirt sleeves rolled up, his hair falling just slightly over his forehead. His presence, as always, was a calming force that anchored her in ways she hadn't imagined possible.

"I was just thinking," Amelia said, a faint smile tugging at her lips. "About how far we've come."

Lucas nodded, his gaze following hers to the fields. "We've come a long way. And we're just getting started."

Amelia's smile grew as she felt a surge of affection for him. They had worked tirelessly over the past months to rebuild what had once seemed like an impossible dream. Together, they had transformed the ranch, not just in terms of land, but in spirit. The renovations to the barn, the stabilization of the estate's financial footing, the effort to restore the community's trust—it had all been a monumental task. But they had persevered, fueled by their shared vision.

"The community's starting to really see what we're doing here," Amelia said, her voice filled with a mix of pride and hope. "The workers have been incredible, the support has been overwhelming. And the media coverage... it's all been positive. It's like we've finally turned the corner."

Lucas leaned against the fence beside her, his arms crossed as he studied the fields. "You've done more than just turn a corner.

You've built something strong here. Not just the ranch. You've built trust."

Amelia looked at him, a sense of gratitude swelling in her chest. "I couldn't have done it without you. I don't think I would have even believed it was possible if I didn't have you by my side."

Lucas's eyes softened. "We did it together. We both had a hand in this."

She let the silence settle between them for a moment, letting the weight of his words sink in. It wasn't just about the ranch, and it wasn't just about the struggles they had faced. It was about the partnership they had built, one that had turned into something far deeper than either of them had expected. Over the months, their relationship had transformed, from a professional one rooted in necessity to something more intimate, something real. Amelia had never imagined that she could find a place like this—a place where she truly felt at home, where she truly felt seen.

Her gaze drifted back to the fields, where the horses grazed peacefully. The sun was beginning to climb higher in the sky, casting a warm, golden glow over everything. It was a new day, a new beginning, and for the first time in a long time, Amelia could see the future.

"I think we're ready to take the next step," she said, her voice steady with conviction.

Lucas turned to look at her, his expression unreadable for a moment. Then, a slight smile tugged at the corners of his lips. "You mean the next step with the ranch, or... with us?"

Amelia felt a sudden surge of warmth flush her cheeks, but she didn't look away. "Both."

His smile widened, and he pushed himself off the fence to stand beside her, their shoulders brushing briefly. "Well, if you're sure, then I'm all in."

Amelia nodded, feeling the weight of his words. This was it—the moment when everything she had worked for, everything she had fought for, had come together. The ranch, Lucas, the community—her life was finally beginning to align in a way she had never dreamed possible. And with Lucas beside her, she knew she could face anything.

"Everything's falling into place," she said softly, her voice full of emotion.

Lucas studied her, his gaze lingering on her face as if searching for something deeper. "It's more than just falling into place, Amelia. You've made this happen. You've rebuilt everything. This—" he gestured toward the ranch, "—this is your legacy. Your father's, too. And it's not just about the land or the animals or the money. It's about the heart of it. It's about what you've done for this place."

Amelia smiled, though the sentiment felt bittersweet. "I wish he could see it. I wish my father could see how we've brought it back. How we've made it what he always dreamed of."

Lucas's expression softened. "I think he would have been proud. You've made him proud."

Her throat tightened. She hadn't realized how much of her heart had been tied to the ranch and the legacy of her father until now. She had spent so many years running away from the past, trying to carve a future that didn't involve the land she'd grown up on. But now, standing here with Lucas by her side, she realized that the past had shaped her and that it was a part of who she was.

"We've come a long way," she whispered, her voice barely audible over the wind. "But we're just getting started, aren't we?"

Lucas turned to face her, a quiet determination in his eyes. "We're just getting started."

With that, they stood together, silently taking in the view, of the future stretching out before them. The ranch was no longer a burden or a fading memory. It was alive again, pulsing with new energy, and new possibilities. And with it, Amelia had found something she had never expected: a home.

It wasn't the home she had imagined for herself all those years ago in the city, but it was more than she had ever dreamed of. It was a life grounded in love, in hard work, in shared dreams. As the sun continued its rise, casting a golden light over the land they had saved together, Amelia knew that this was where she was meant to be.

Her father's legacy was restored. Her own future was just beginning.

And with Lucas by her side, nothing seemed impossible.

32

The Simple Life

The sun was setting, casting a golden hue across the ranch. Amelia stood by the fence, gazing out at the land she had once believed she would leave behind forever. The horses grazed peacefully in the fields, their movements slow and graceful. The distant hills were bathed in warm light, and the evening air was rich with the scent of fresh grass and earth.

A contented sigh escaped her lips. This was the life she had once feared, the life she had avoided for so long. But now, standing here, surrounded by the land that had been her family's legacy, Amelia couldn't imagine living anywhere else.

Lucas walked up beside her, his boots crunching on the gravel as he approached. He offered her a warm smile, his eyes crinkling at the corners. He had always been a man of few words, but his presence spoke volumes. The connection between them had deepened in ways that neither of them could have expected. They had built something together—something real.

"Beautiful, isn't it?" Lucas asked, his voice low and steady.

Amelia nodded, her gaze never leaving the horizon. "It is. I never thought I would come to love it like this."

Lucas leaned against the fence beside her, his arms crossed, looking out over the land with a quiet satisfaction. "You've made it yours. This place... it's different now. It's alive again."

The ranch had been through so much in the past months. The financial struggles, the threats from the developers, and the hard work they'd put in to restore everything—it had been overwhelming. But in the end, it had all paid off. The ranch was thriving, the community was coming together, and the future was looking brighter than ever. It wasn't just the land that had been revitalized; it was Amelia's heart, too.

"I can't believe we did it," Amelia whispered, more to herself than to Lucas.

"We did it together," he corrected softly, turning to face her. "You were the one who made it happen, Amelia. You fought for this place. And for your father's legacy."

She met his gaze, her heart swelling with a mixture of pride and love. Lucas had been her rock throughout this entire process. When she had doubted herself, when the pressure seemed too much to bear, he had been there—steadfast and patient. They had spent countless hours working side by side, from the crack of dawn to the late hours of the night, rebuilding the ranch and their future.

But it wasn't just the work that had brought them closer. It was the quiet moments they shared—the evenings spent under the stars, the conversations that ran deep, the laughter that filled the empty spaces between them. They had found something more than just a business partnership. They had found love. True, unspoken, simple love.

"I don't think I ever truly understood what it meant to be grounded until now," Amelia said, her voice soft, almost contemplative. "All those years in the city, chasing success, trying to prove something to myself... I never realized how much I had missed. How much I needed something like this."

"You were always so focused on the future," Lucas said, his voice tinged with understanding. "But you've built something real now. Something that's not just about what's ahead, but about what you have right here, right now."

She smiled, glancing at him. "You're right. I was so consumed by my career, by everything I thought I needed to succeed. But I've come to realize that true success isn't measured by how much money you make or how many accomplishments you have. It's about the people who stand beside you, the love you give and receive, and the way you live your life."

Lucas stepped closer, his presence warm and comforting. He reached out, gently brushing a strand of hair from her face. "And now we have each other. This place. Our future. Everything."

Amelia's heart skipped a beat as she looked up at him. There was something undeniably comforting about him, something that made her feel like she had finally found a place where she truly belonged. His hands, calloused from years of hard work, had a strength to them that grounded her, and his eyes, so often reserved and guarded, were filled with an intensity that made her feel seen. Underneath the rugged exterior, she had come to realize that Lucas was a man capable of incredible tenderness, of love that didn't need to be spoken but was felt deeply.

"I never thought I could be happy here," she confessed, her voice barely above a whisper. "I thought I'd outgrow this life, leave it all behind for something bigger, something better. But now... I can't imagine being anywhere else."

Lucas's expression softened, and for a moment, all the words between them seemed unnecessary. His hand found hers, and they stood together in the silence, letting the beauty of the evening wash over them. The steady sound of the wind in the trees, the soft rustle of the leaves, and the distant call of birds created a symphony of peace around them.

"I feel the same," Lucas said, his voice barely audible. "I thought I'd always be tied to this place, never able to leave. But now... I see something new, something worth fighting for. And it's with you."

Amelia's heart fluttered at his words. It was in moments like these, when the world seemed to stop spinning for just a second, that she realized how much she had grown, how much they had both grown. They had built something together, something real. And despite the challenges, despite the doubts and fears that had tried to hold them back, they had made it through. Together.

The sound of hooves echoed from the barn, breaking the stillness. Lucas's horse was ready, and so was Amelia's. She turned to him with a smile. "Shall we?"

He smiled back, his eyes glinting with that same warmth she had come to love. "After you, Miss Pierce."

They mounted their horses, the reins in their hands, ready for whatever lay ahead. Together, they were unstoppable. The future was theirs to build, one step at a time. And as they rode through the fields, the wind in their hair, the world around them felt full of promise, full of life, full of love.

The simple life was everything Amelia had ever needed—and now, it was hers.

33

A Forever Love

The sun was setting over the horizon, casting a warm glow over the sprawling ranch. Amelia stood by the barn, her hand resting gently on the wooden fence, watching the colors of the sky shift from gold to soft pinks and purples. The air was still, carrying the scent of fresh hay and earth, grounding her in the present moment. She had come so far in such a short time, and yet, it felt as though the past, the struggles, and the uncertainty were just distant memories. Everything had changed in ways she could have never predicted.

Lucas was working nearby, leading one of the horses back to the stables, his tall figure moving with purpose, a quiet confidence in every step. He was a man of few words, but in his presence, Amelia had learned more about herself than she ever could have imagined. She had come to realize that true love didn't come with grand gestures or sweeping declarations. It was built in the quiet moments—the ones spent side by side, sharing in the joys and challenges of life.

The sound of hooves on the gravel grew louder as Lucas approached. Amelia turned to meet his gaze, feeling her heart flutter as their eyes met. He stopped beside her, his expression softening as he leaned against the fence next to her.

"You know, I never thought I'd be the kind of person to settle down," Lucas said, his voice low and thoughtful. "I always thought I'd be tied to this land, tied to the ranch, with no real place for anyone else. But when you came back... everything changed."

Amelia smiled, her heart swelling with affection. "I think we both had our doubts about what this place—this life—could be," she said, her voice gentle. "I didn't want to come back here either. But somehow, we've made it work. We've made it ours."

Lucas nodded, his eyes scanning the horizon. "It hasn't been easy. But the more I think about it, the more I realize that this place, this land, isn't just a part of my past. It's our future. And I couldn't have imagined building that future with anyone but you."

Her heart skipped a beat at his words. Amelia turned to face him fully, her hand brushing against his as they stood there in the fading light. For so long, she had fought the idea of belonging to something so deeply rooted, something so unyielding as this ranch, this life. But in Lucas, she had found a love that had opened her eyes to a whole new world—one where love wasn't about what you owned or what you had achieved, but about who you were with and how deeply you cared for them.

"Lucas," she whispered, her voice shaky with emotion. "When I first came back, I had no idea how much I needed this. How much I needed you."

He met her gaze, and for a moment, the world around them seemed to stop. There was no need for words between them anymore. The connection they had built over the months was palpable, woven into every glance, every touch. They had both come to terms with the parts of themselves they had tried to suppress—the fears, the doubts, the insecurities—and had found strength in each other.

"You don't have to say anything more," Lucas replied softly. "I know."

And with that, Amelia felt a deep peace settle within her. The uncertainty, the fear that had once held her back, began to melt away. In Lucas, she had found not just a partner, but a home. A place to be herself, to trust, to love.

As the sun dipped below the horizon, casting the world in a deep amber hue, Lucas took her hand in his, his fingers intertwining with hers. The quiet of the evening wrapped around them like a blanket, and for the first time in a long time, Amelia felt the weight of the world lift from her shoulders.

Together, they walked towards the stables, the familiar sounds of the ranch—horses snorting, the rustle of the wind through the trees—filling the air. But now, it felt different. It wasn't just a place she was passing through—it was home.

"You know," Amelia said, breaking the comfortable silence between them, "I used to think that love was about finding the perfect person, the one who could give you everything you ever wanted."

Lucas chuckled softly, his grip tightening around her hand. "You mean, you thought love was supposed to be perfect?"

Amelia smiled, shaking her head. "Something like that. But now I realize it's not about perfection. It's about building something real, something lasting. And that's what we've done. We've created something strong—together."

Lucas stopped walking and turned to face her, his eyes soft but intense. "I don't know what the future holds, but I do know this—I want to spend it with you. You're more than I could have ever hoped for."

Her breath caught in her throat. He was always so calm, so composed, but in this moment, she could see the raw emotion in his eyes, the depth of his feelings for her. The realization that they were finally in sync—that they had truly found each other—washed over her like a wave.

"I want that too," Amelia whispered, her voice thick with emotion. "I've never felt more sure of anything in my life."

The silence between them felt like a promise, unspoken but understood. The world could be chaotic, and uncertain, but in this moment, Amelia knew that with Lucas by her side, everything would be okay. They had come through the storm—

together. And now, they were ready to build something even stronger.

As they continued walking toward the stables, their hands still intertwined, Amelia allowed herself to look ahead, not just at the ranch, but at the future. The road ahead was theirs to shape, filled with possibilities they had never imagined.

And for the first time, she was not afraid of what the future held. She had found her place—not just on the land, but with the man who had shown her that love wasn't about the life you left behind, but the one you created together.

"Let's do this," she said, her voice steady and full of determination.

Lucas smiled, his eyes sparkling with the same confidence that had drawn her to him from the start. "Together," he replied, his voice full of conviction.

And as they walked into the stables, side by side, Amelia realized that everything she had ever needed had been right here all along: a love that was real, a future to look forward to, and the man who would be there through it all.

The sun had set, but for the first time in a long while, Amelia felt like she was exactly where she was meant to be.

34

The Final Chapter

The air was thick with anticipation as the first rays of sunlight crept over the horizon, casting long shadows across the ranch. Amelia stood on the porch of the house she had once been so reluctant to return to but now felt like home. She had never imagined this moment—standing here with Lucas, her heart full, the future uncertain but full of promise. It was a moment she could never have foreseen when she first arrived at the ranch, carrying with her the weight of a life that had never quite fit her.

"Are you sure you're ready for this?" Lucas's voice broke through her thoughts, low and steady, a reflection of the quiet strength he always carried with him. He was standing a few feet away, looking out across the land as though it were his lifeblood, his gaze fixed on the horizon, on what lay beyond.

Amelia turned toward him, the early morning sunlight illuminating his features, casting a golden glow over his rugged face. She had come to know him in so many ways—the tough exterior, the vulnerable heart hidden beneath, and the unwavering commitment to the land that had shaped both him and the life they were now creating together. He had become her partner in every sense of the word, a man she could trust with her heart and soul.

"I'm ready," Amelia replied softly, but there was a sense of finality in her voice. The words carried a weight that went beyond just the decision to stay. It was the culmination of everything they had built together, everything they had fought for. Her life, once filled with ambition and a deep sense of isolation in the city, had shifted, and blossomed into something new. With Lucas by her side, she was ready for anything.

"Ready for what?" Lucas turned, his gaze now focused on her as if he could read the depth of her thoughts.

Amelia took a step forward, the cool morning breeze brushing against her face, and for a moment, everything else faded. The house, the ranch, the distant hills—it was just her and Lucas at that moment, standing together, both uncertain and certain all at once. She walked up to him and took his hand, her fingers brushing against his as their gazes locked.

"Ready for everything. For whatever comes next," she said, her voice steady. "We've come this far, and we're only just getting started. We have a future to build, Lucas. A future that's ours."

He smiled at her, the lines of his face softening, and for the first time, she saw the full extent of the man he was—strong, but vulnerable, unyielding, yet open to the possibility of a life he had never imagined before. The journey they had taken together had transformed them both. It had tested their love, their commitment, and ultimately had brought them to a place of undeniable connection.

"Then let's build it," Lucas said quietly, squeezing her hand as if sealing the promise. There was no more doubt in his eyes, no hesitation in his voice.

But Amelia knew that the path ahead wouldn't be easy. The struggles they had overcome—the debts, the pressure from outside forces, the tension between their worlds—were not over. But now, they faced them together. They had fought for this, for the life they had chosen, and they weren't going to stop now.

"I've been thinking," Amelia began, her voice dropping, a flicker of uncertainty crossing her mind despite her resolve. "We've got so much to rebuild here, not just with the ranch, but with the community. My family, the people who've always been part of this place—they need to know we're in this together."

Lucas nodded, his eyes never leaving hers. "They already know. You've shown them more than anyone could have expected. This place is in your blood, Amelia. You don't have to prove anything."

She smiled, but a small part of her was still afraid. Afraid of letting go of the person she once was, the person who was always chasing after more, seeking approval and recognition. The city had demanded so much from her—ambition, perfection, success—but here, on the ranch, she had learned what truly mattered. And it was with Lucas, in the quiet moments, that she realized the truth: she didn't need to be anything other than who she was.

"I never thought I could find peace in a place like this," Amelia said, her voice low and soft. "But with you, I'm not just surviving. I'm living. And I want to keep living like this, by your side."

Lucas reached for her, his touch gentle but firm as he pulled her closer. "You don't have to worry, Amelia. I'm not going anywhere. And neither are you. We'll do this together, step by step. We'll make sure this ranch stands, not just for us, but for everyone who believes in it."

She looked up into his eyes, and for the first time, she realized that the weight she had carried for so long—the uncertainty, the fear—was gone. It had been replaced with something stronger, something lasting. Love. Not the kind of love that was possessive or obsessive, but the kind that allowed both people to stand on equal ground, side by side.

"I love you," she whispered, the words feeling like a breath she had held for far too long.

Lucas's expression softened as he cupped her face in his hands, his thumb brushing against her cheek. "I love you too, more than you know."

The world around them felt still, but Amelia knew that everything had changed. They had changed. The ranch, the life they were building—it all had a new purpose now. And whatever challenges lay ahead, they would face them together.

As the sun continued to rise, casting its golden light over the land, Amelia knew this was just the beginning. The hard work, the sacrifices, the love—they would build a future that would last, not just for them, but for everyone who called the ranch home.

The future was theirs to create, and Amelia was ready to take the first step. Hand in hand with Lucas, she stepped forward, leaving behind the uncertainties of the past and embracing the life they had built together.

This was their time. Their love. And nothing could stand in their way.

35

From Skyscrapers to Stables

The morning sun crept slowly over the horizon, casting a soft golden glow across the sprawling ranch. Amelia stood on the porch of the modest farmhouse, looking out over the vast landscape, the morning mist still clinging to the earth. The wind carried with it the scent of fresh hay and earth—scents she had come to love over the past year. It was a far cry from the bustling streets of New York, the clatter of the city now a distant memory. Here, in the silence of the countryside, she had found a peace that seemed almost unnatural after years of living in constant chaos.

She took a deep breath, filling her lungs with the clean, crisp air. It had been a long road to get here. When she first arrived at the ranch, she had been a stranger to this way of life, burdened by obligations and haunted by the weight of her father's legacy. But everything had changed. The responsibilities, the tensions, the constant running—it had all led her to this moment, a moment of clarity.

Amelia turned her gaze toward the stables in the distance. It was where she had spent countless hours over the past year, learning, growing, and sometimes struggling to adapt. The ranch had become her life, and the stables, once a place of unfamiliarity, now felt like home. But it wasn't just the land that had changed her—it was Lucas.

The sound of footsteps behind her made her turn. Lucas stood at the edge of the porch, his presence solid and comforting as ever. His eyes met hers, a quiet understanding passing between them without the need for words. He had become everything she never thought she needed—a partner in every sense of the word. He had shown her the way through the storm, not just for the ranch, but for her own heart.

"You're up early," Lucas said, his voice low, almost a whisper, as if not wanting to disturb the peace that surrounded them. He approached her slowly, his eyes scanning the horizon, his hand resting on the porch railing.

Amelia smiled, her heart warming at the sight of him. Over the past year, she had come to know him not just as the man who had taught her the ways of the ranch, but as someone she could trust, someone who had shown her what it truly meant to live. The hard edges he had worn when they first met had softened, revealing a man of depth, of scars, of dreams. He was no longer just the rugged rancher who had once resisted her city ways—he was her equal, her partner, and the man who had stolen her heart in ways she never thought possible.

"I couldn't sleep," she admitted, her voice barely above a

whisper. "I was thinking about everything—how far we've come."

Lucas stepped closer, his presence a steadying force. He reached out, brushing a stray strand of hair from her face, his touch gentle but firm. "It's been a hell of a journey," he said, his gaze never leaving hers. "But you've done it. You've built something here. We've built something."

Her heart swelled at his words. She had never thought she would be capable of running a ranch, much less making it thrive. Yet, here she was, standing at the threshold of a new life, a life that had grown from the seeds of uncertainty and the promise of a future she had only begun to understand. The past year had been filled with challenges, disagreements, and moments of doubt, but it had also been a year of growth—both for the ranch and for her.

"Do you ever miss it?" she asked, her voice tinged with curiosity. "The city, I mean. The skyscrapers, the endless buzz..."

Lucas chuckled softly, his eyes flickering with amusement. "I used to think I did," he admitted, shaking his head. "But every day here, it feels more and more like I'm exactly where I'm supposed to be. And as for you—" He paused, taking her hand in his. "You've made this place feel like home, Amelia."

Her heart fluttered at the sincerity in his words. There was no trace of doubt in his voice, no hesitation. The life they had created together was real, and it was beautiful.

"I think you're right," she said quietly. "For the first time, I can honestly say that I feel like this is where I belong."

They stood there for a moment, both lost in the peace of the morning, the quiet only broken by the distant sounds of the ranch animals. The decision to stay, to build a life here together, had been one of the hardest decisions she had ever made. But it had been the right one. The fear that had once gripped her heart—fear of change, fear of failure, fear of losing herself—had dissipated. She had found herself in the most unexpected of places: among the stables, on the land she had once dreaded, with Lucas by her side.

"I've been thinking," Amelia said, her voice filled with resolve. "About the future, about what's next for us."

Lucas raised an eyebrow, his attention fully on her now. "What do you mean?"

"I mean..." She hesitated for a moment, gathering her thoughts. "We've rebuilt the ranch. But what if we could expand it? Not just for the land, but for the people. We could create something that gives back to the community. Something that lasts."

Lucas studied her for a moment as if weighing her words. Then, a slow smile spread across his face, his eyes lighting up with approval. "I've always believed in this place. But I never thought we'd be able to give something like that back. You think we could?"

Amelia nodded. "Yes. We've already proven that we can make

it work. Now, it's time to think bigger. We could do something that not only honors my father's legacy but brings new life to this area. Maybe even create a space where people can experience the ranch life—be part of something real."

Lucas looked at her with a mixture of admiration and something deeper—something more powerful. "You've come a long way, Amelia. From the city girl who never wanted to come back to the ranch to the woman who wants to make it thrive. I'm proud of you."

Her chest tightened with emotion. She had worked so hard to earn his respect, to build something worthy of the land and the family legacy. Now, she didn't just have a ranch to be proud of. She had a future, a purpose, and a man who believed in her.

"We'll make it work," she said, more confidently than she had ever spoken before. "Together."

Lucas leaned in, pressing a gentle kiss to her forehead. "Together," he echoed, his voice full of promise.

The morning sun climbed higher, and as the warmth of the day touched the earth, Amelia knew that whatever challenges lay ahead, they would face them side by side. The ranch, once a symbol of her past, had become the foundation of her future. The skyscrapers of the city were no longer a distant dream to chase. This was where she belonged, with Lucas, on this land that had become hers in ways she never imagined.

With their hands intertwined, they turned toward the stables, ready to continue building their life. Together, they had proven that love could grow in the most unexpected places, that transformation was possible, and that true wealth wasn't measured in buildings or bank accounts—it was found in the strength of their love and the land they had made their own.

9 788165 564179

Printed at Repro India Ltd.